Soul Connection

ADDICTION · RECOVERY · SOBRIETY

- HANNAH COLLINS -

Witchwork Publishing

Soul Connection: Addiction – Recovery - Sobriety
Copyright © Hannah Collins. First published 2021

Hannah Collins asserts the moral right to be identified
as the author of Soul Connection: Addiction – Recovery - Sobriety
Copyright © Witchwork Publishing

All rights reserved. No part of this publication may be reproduced, stored in a retrieval system or transmitted in any form or by any means, mechanical, electronic, photocopying, recording or otherwise, without the prior written permission of the author.

This book and any associated materials, suggestions and advice are intended to give general information only. The author expressly disclaims all liability to any person arising directly or indirectly from the use of or for any errors or omissions in this book. The adoption and application of the information in this book is at the readers' discretion and is his or her sole responsibility.

All names of persons and personal identifying details mentioned in this book have been changed to protect their privacy.

Soul Connection: Addiction – Recovery – Sobriety Hannah Collins
ISBN: 978-0-646-84212-7

Edited: Karen Crombie - Exact Editing
Cover Design: Joanne Tapodi Creative
Author photograph: Philippe Flatt - Image Technique Photography

by Hannah Collins

In Business Together: Negotiating The Intimate Relationship
And The Business Relationship
How To Overcome Your Fear Of Writing: eBook
Soul Connection: Addiction–Recovery–Sobriety

For my wife,
Thank you for giving me the loving, supportive happiness
that allows me to dig deep into my subconscious and heal.
-Hannah Collins

For my sons,
I'm sorry for the unhealed parts of me that in turn hurt you.
It was never a lack of love for you, only a lack of love for my Self.
-Teresa Shanti

The cover illustration by Joanne Tapodi represents the three parts of the book:

- **Part one:** childhood, family dysfunction and alcoholism, as represented by waves of a stormy sea, here we can think of emotions of feeling lost, overwhelmed, a sense of drowning.

- **Part two:** Time in rehab as represented by thick clouds, here we see feelings of cloudy thoughts and emotions, confusion, being caught in a haze, trying to find yourself in a fog.

- **Part three:** Leaving hospital and living a sober life. Here the lines are finer, representing feeling lighter and less heavy; you are the bird soaring into an open sky towards the sun, relishing the warmth and new opportunities. There is a heart shape in the bird that represents the 'Soul Connection'.

She fell
She crashed
She broke
She cried
She crawled
She hurt
She surrendered

And then . . .
She rose again.

From Beautiful Minds Anonymous.
A book of poems.

Soul Connection
ADDICTION · RECOVERY · SOBRIETY

Introduction

My name is Hannah Collins and I'm an alcoholic and drug addict. I know from personal experience that alcoholics and drug addicts lie, cheat, steal, and manipulate. They engage in risky behaviour, have no impulse control and no conscience. And until they admit they have a problem and choose sobriety, addiction will take them to one of three places: jail, hospital or a grave.

When I talk about the years of my alcohol and drug use someone inevitably asks, "What made you stop?" "What happened?" "Why did you give it up?" "How did you stop?" or "What's your story?"

The daughter of my friend and neighbour was getting married. Ours was a farming community and the 'City Girl' was coming home for her wedding. We, her friends and relatives, lent a hand on the big day working in the farmhouse kitchen, putting hay bales out on the back lawn for seating, decorating the front gate with wild flowers, making up beds for the overnight guests and providing extra plates, glasses, cups, and cutlery.

I don't remember much about the day. I know I spent most of the morning *preparing vegetables, whipping cream, decorating sponges and making endless cups of tea. I helped ferry food out to the decorated tables on the back lawn under the trees. But I have no memory of the ceremony or the evening celebrations. The next day we'd arranged to go back down the valley and help with the clean-up. As we sat over cups of tea I casually suggested the hair-of-the-dog to clear the head and steady the hands.*

I was cried down. There was much shaking of heads, comments about having overdone it last night and swearing off drink altogether. But I wanted a drink. I couldn't think of anything but needing a drink. I couldn't settle or keep up with the conversation, my mind was racing, spinning, wondering how I could have a drink without drawing attention to myself. I was desperate.

It did register that I was the only one wanting a drink. I understood I was acting differently than everyone else. And as I sat on the back steps of my friend's house, I admitted to myself that I had a problem.

That wasn't the first time I'd seen my drinking and drug use as different from others. The thought that I was an alcoholic and drug addict had lingered in the back of my mind for years. But following the wedding, I took action and without discussing it with anyone, I phoned Alcoholics Anonymous and learned the time and place of my nearest A.A. meeting. For twenty-odd years I've not raised a glass of alcohol at a wedding, a celebration, in company or in secret. And I've never bought or used an illegal substance.

I went cold-turkey after the wedding and despite my years of addiction, not drinking or using drugs was the easy part. The hard part was confronting the emotions from my childhood sexual abuse, the overwhelming feelings of shame, guilt and humiliation. Added to this was the trauma of five years of physical and mental abuse from a coercive bullying partner in a violent relationship.

Recovery wasn't only about the damage I'd done to myself but also about the damage I caused others, especially my two children. Consumed by my emotional pain and the escalation of my addiction, I'd abandoned the responsibility of being a mother. I'd become unable to consider anyone else's needs but my own.

Recovery is a long and difficult journey, physically, mentally and emotionally. For weeks and months there are cravings, flashbacks, memories, nightmares, anxiety and feeling emotionally overwhelmed. Feeling out of control from panic attacks and emotional pain, I was on constant alert fighting off the thought that a drink or drug would take away all the pain.

I began with childhood sexual abuse counselling and then began dealing with the coercive, abusive adult relationships I'd been drawn to. Over the years I've used many types of therapy, including Gestalt, Journaling, Dreamwork, Cathartic Writing, Psychotherapy, Inner Child, Meditation and Hypnotherapy. I worked the 12-Steps and returned to my Pagan Spiritual practice. I used ritual and Wiccan tools like tarot cards, crystals, healing herbs and remedies like Bach Flowers. I discovered 'The Artist's Way'.

When I was six months sober I was accepted into the residential, government-sponsored, Alcoholics Anonymous rehab program. Based on the 12-Steps, abstinence and connection with your Higher Self, the four-week program educated addicts on the disease of addiction, held daily group therapy, Alcoholics Anonymous or Narcotics Anonymous Meetings and one-on-one counselling with relationship and family-based therapists.

An essential part of my recovery and healing was finding and making amends to my sons. These were the two people I had hurt the most and it was very difficult and incredibly painful listening to their childhood experiences and becoming aware of how much trauma I had caused. I'll always be grateful they gave me the opportunity to talk openly about my addiction and to address the damage I'd caused them.

It might surprise you to learn I'm also grateful to my disease. Without it I might never have been able to deal with the issues of the childhood molestation I'd endured or the abusive and controlling relationships I was addicted to. In recovery I was able to resolve our family co-dependency patterns, change my limiting self-beliefs and forgive myself. Through recovery and sobriety I've become a more resilient person. I'm more open and forgiving, less judgemental and more empathetic. I can now look in the mirror and say out loud, *I love you.*

I wanted to share my story as a gift of hope to others on a similar journey. This is a story of victory over adversity, from victim to more than a mere survivor. I'm living a fully authentic life, knowing my Soul Path is connection and that writing my stories are my Life Purpose.

This is a story of healing and it's in that spirit I thank you for reading my work, my words, and please share this book with anyone you believe needs to be inspired and given hope.

Goddess, grant me the serenity to accept the things I cannot change.
The courage to change the things I can
And the wisdom to know the difference.

Hannah Collins, Author

WEEK ONE

I admitted I was powerless over alcohol, that my life had become unmanageable.

1

The bus trip is never-ending. I feel I've been a prisoner of this sticky leather seat for days and days, not hours. I'm both in a hurry and reluctant to arrive. The fear in my belly is a broiling mass that threatens to erupt in a river of vomit. I'm feeling motion sickness and there's nothing more embarrassing than leaving a damp, smelly, sick bag when exiting your chosen form of transport.

I'd been on the hospital waiting list for three months and I'm still not prepared for today. The time seems to have flown by and I'm not sure what to expect. There have been stories from others who've been through the program, some encouraging, making me glad I applied and others that added to my fear.

But I remain firm in my decision. I need to do more than just stop drinking and using drugs. I want more than being in recovery forever. There has to be something beyond recovery, not just hovering in that no-man's-land, *not-a-drunk* but not being cured either. I'm hoping the hospital program will give me the knowledge and tools to remain sober, and also to stop feeling like a frightened little girl who's pretending to be a grown-up.

The bus pulls off the main road into a tree-lined lane and on through a rusty pair of wrought iron gates. We park in a hiss of air brakes and I leave my sticky seat on rubbery legs to walk down the aisle. From the open doorway I catch my first glimpse of the historic hospital.

Shabby and rundown, with a tired iron roof and open verandas, the purpose-built convalescent home for returning shell-shocked soldiers sits in a large acreage of well-tended grounds and gardens. Under her current reincarnation the hospital is considered the country's most successful rehab facility for the treatment of alcohol addiction and drug dependency.

I take two quick breaths, take a firm hold of my bag and walking with purpose, head down the footpath to the sign saying *Admissions*. Would I have been so confident had I known I was about to sign myself into a psychiatric hospital as a voluntary patient for thirty days?

The admission office is tucked just inside the main doors and my impression is of a small, dark, cave-like room. My eyes need to adjust from the bright afternoon sunlight and I'm still suffering from the effects of the motion sickness. The nurse is in a regulation white uniform and she greets me with a smile. I'm given a quick rundown of the admissions procedure, a map of the hospital including the grounds, a list of the staff and their positions, and a timetable.

We begin with a mandatory bag search which comes as a surprise as I hadn't given much thought to the rules. My bag is emptied onto a low shelf and the nurse proceeds to pick up and shake the items, including underclothing, summer pants, a shirt, some T-shirts, my favourite cable-knit cardigan, and an extra pair of strappy sandals, plus toiletries. I also have books, tarot cards, a wishing candle, box of matches, journal, pens and my go-every-where bear Maude.

It feels weird watching the nurse take a particular interest in the toiletries. Maybe people bring in alcohol-flavoured toothpaste or soap with hidden drugs. My new moon candle and box of matches are confiscated. It seems I might accidentally burn down the hospital. The tarot deck raises the nurse's eyebrows but after a moment of indecision she says nothing. Maude gets squeezed from her ears to her fur toes but nothing is found and I'm told I can repack.

We sit either side of the small desk and the nurse opens a manila folder. She checks my personal details and there's more raised eyebrows about my answer to the question of religion. I'm Pagan. It seems the nurse hasn't heard of that and she looks up and tells me there's never been a pagan patient in the hospital. I wonder if, like gays, the Pagans haven't felt safe to admit that on the application forms.

Next, I handed a typed sheet of hospital rules. Again, something I hadn't given much thought.

Under the threat of instant dismissal.
- No **buying, selling** or **using** alcohol or drugs.
- No **gang patches or related insignia** on clothing.
- No verbal or **physical intimidation** toward hospital staff, visitors or fellow patients.
- Nil tolerance for **profanity.**
- **No romantic liaisons, sexual relationships or special friendships** between hospital staff or fellow patients.

And at the bottom of the page, in bold print, is a blunt warning:

The local villagers can tell at a glance who is a tourist and who is a hospital resident. If any patient attempts to enter either the hotel or bottle store, causes a disturbance or becomes a public nuisance, the hospital will be informed and immediate action taken.

Soul Connection

Having read the page I'm asked to initial the bottom. I'm handed a new form. This is the formal agreement between the hospital and myself. I run my eye down page and reach for the pen. It all seems standard, the usual jargon, the hospital will provide this and that, the patient agrees. And just as I'm about to sign, I notice several sentences in small print at the bottom. Administrated by the department of mental health . . . Psychiatric Hospital. . . volunteer patient.

My first thought is that this will be recorded on my medical records forever. Anyone can see it!

My hand hovers in the air as a hundred thoughts run through my head. Does being an alcoholic automatically make me a psychiatric patient? I've always felt like an outsider, never fitting in, always being over-talkative, over-emotional, doing crazy things, losing my temper, being disruptive at school, argumentative, getting into fights, being aggressive. I know my mother dished out pills to calm me down around birthdays and Christmas. There were always these hints about me being uncontrollable as a child, nervy and excitable.

But where did that leave all the work I'd done over the last six months, the endless headaches, aching bones, racing heart, nightmares and panic attacks? I glance at the nurse sitting stoically in front of me and then down at the paper. All that filling out of application forms, adding referral letters from the doctor, the sexual abuse counsellor, drug and alcohol clinic and the final indignity, my own handwritten letter recommending myself and why I should be considered.

Bottom line, I need to be here, I want to change my life, I want to get sober and stay sober. And I need help to do that. Taking a fresh grip on the pen I scribble my name at the bottom of the page before I change my mind.

2

Any architectural brilliance of the historical building is wasted on me as I hurry down the corridor after the briskly striding nurse. There is, however, as we pass, evidence of the run down nature and lack of general maintenance in the cracked floor-to-ceiling tiles, water stains, a buckled and broken window frame. Overall, there's an air of neglect.

The main corridor branches off in both directions from the central nurse's station. The left leads to where we are headed; the women's dorm and to the right is the men's. The fully tiled corridor is reminiscent of running for a train down a long, echoing underground railway platform. Through the evenly spaced windows I get a peek of people strolling or sitting, tidy rose gardens, a water feature, tall trees and a volleyball court.

We halt in front of a pair of frosted glass double doors and the nurse shoulders them open. I'm ushered into a large room with a dozen white, iron-framed, single beds. Each bed has a small chest of drawers, shaded reading lamp, white cotton coverlet, two thin pillows and a blanket folded neatly across the foot. For a moment I think I've wandered into the home of Snow White and the Seven Dwarfs.

I'm not the first to arrive. There's bags and open suitcases on several beds, one littered with discarded clothing, an array of toiletries and a pink hairdryer. I'm told to choose a bed. I walk the length of the room and put my bag on the corner bed, while trying to come to terms with the shared sleeping arrangements. My clothes divide easily between the three drawers, I stack the books on top and place my shoes beneath the bed. I push the tarot deck discreetly under the pillows and perch Maude the bear on top.

I'm reminded of my childhood bedroom and sharing with my sister. Twin beds with matching candlewick bedspreads, a large, shared chest of drawers between under the window, so we had to roll on our sides out of bed to see each other. We had framed pictures above the beds; mine was a prima ballerina, arms in a circle above her head, in a white tutu. My sister's was a line of cygnets with feather headdresses, balancing on pointe.

I don't remember spending time in our bedroom playing, usually we were shooed outside onto the wide covered veranda with our younger siblings to stop from getting under our mother's feet. While I know this and can recall it, I always think of myself as being alone, an only child, not the eldest of six.

I make myself comfortable on the bed and taking my journal, make a quick sketch of the room. I write a few words around the funny line drawing and then become engrossed in recording the bus trip, my first impression of the hospital, the nurse, and signing myself into a psych hospital for thirty days.

Sitting in the quiet of the sizeable space I can feel myself as two parts. On the outside I feel alert and watchful, the act of pretending everything is under control. Meanwhile, inside I feel like that frightened little girl ready to run. It's not a new feeling. I often feel like a fraud, a child dressed in adult clothing, hiding secrets, feeling guilty and ashamed, waiting to be found out.

When I hear voices and the clatter of shoes in the corridor I close my journal and wait. A group of young women breeze in through the doors, filling the room with noise, each heading for their bed. They continue to chat until someone notices me at the other end of the room and then there's silence. I realise I'm the oldest, these women are closer to my sons in age, certainly no more than very early thirties while I'm in my late forties. We're a generation apart and I suddenly feel old.

I say "Hi," and introduce myself, walking toward them, wearing what I hope is a welcoming smile. The women come forward, some offering a hand, others seeming to offer a hug but their arms never quite making it around me. It's a little awkward, everyone's a bit shy and hesitant. Everyone says their name but I forget them almost immediately. There's a rush of babbled information; where we've come from, what we think so far, punctuated by self-conscious bursts of laughter.

Abruptly, the double doors swing open and the nurse appears with a new youngster. She introduces Becky and after a silence that goes on for too long, I jump in and point to the last bed next to mine. Becky continues to stand just inside the doors, her large suitcase held protectively in front of her with both hands. When she finally moves forward the group dissolves into busyness.

The deafening clanging of the bell in the corridor gives me a fright, making me jump. It's the five o'clock dinner bell. While it seems very early for an evening meal, there's an A.A. Meeting in the village hall to attend before lights out at ten. As I slip my feet back into my sandals and push my journal under the pillow, I realise this is how it's going to be from now on, a daily regimen of bells and timetables.

The renovated dining room hasn't lost any of its architectural beauty.

It's bright and airy with large picture windows looking out across the grounds and rose gardens. There's nostalgic black and white photographs of nurses in long uniforms with white aprons and winged caps, groups of soldiers sitting outside in cane chairs, plus an old square-shaped ambulance with a painted red cross on the back doors.

The room is crowded to near capacity and after the quiet of the dorm the noise is a little overwhelming. I join the queue creeping toward the heat-lamp servery staffed by women in long aprons and unattractive disposable hairnets. When I reach the counter I take one of the thick white dinner plates and a set of cutlery from the metal canisters. I try not to gawk but there's so many people and these are just patients; the staff have their own dining room.

There are four people assigned to each small cloth-covered table, all of different age, hair colour, height, weight, and dress sense. Some look like they've just come from the office, others from the streets, men with shaved heads, tattooed necks and arms, some with fashionable haircuts, long or trimmed beards. I have to shake myself mentally and remind myself we're all addicts.

I walk around the tables, plate in hand, looking for the table number I've been allotted according to the seating plan. I take my place at the table in the back corner and introduce myself to the woman and two young men already seated. When I question the seating plan, I'm told its hospital policy to stop the formation of cliques and special friends that might become romantic or make divisions along race, religion, sex or political lines. We're here to learn how to find *sameness* not *differences*.

We eat in silence, unlike most of the other tables. There's laughter and raised voices over a comfortable general hum of conversation. People get up and help themselves to tea or coffee from the urns of boiling water set out on the long narrow table against the far wall. There's also baskets of warm bread rolls, dishes of wrapped butter and other condiments.

The room has a congenial feel, everyone appears to be getting on and I feel more relaxed than I have in weeks. I haven't been sleeping as I've been keyed up about coming to the hospital, worried about the program and what we'd be asked to do. I'd promised myself I'd participate fully, do everything required, and only walk away if it was suggested I was an alcoholic because I was a lesbian.

The woman next to me offers to take my empty plate and bring us back dessert. She seems pleasant, very genuine and I pass my plate, returning her smile. This is a very different meal to the ones I had as a child. Sitting around the red Formica table, covered in a multi-coloured, striped seersucker tablecloth, mum on the kitchen side and dad at the head, ready to clip the ear of any child who spoke out of turn. There was no speaking allowed at the table. Dad's moods were unpredictable; he might tell a joke or share a work story one night and lash out the next. There was no vegetable that remained uneaten, even if you had to sit there all night. I still have food issues when eating at a table.

The dining room begins to empty out. Chairs are scraped back, plates dropped into one of the plastic tubs filled with soapy water, cups and saucers in another, cutlery in a smaller tub. I say goodnight and goodbye to my tablemates, as I'll be sitting at a different table with three new people at breakfast.

3

The corridor bell is loud enough to wake the soundest sleeper. I wake, still fatigued from an unfamiliar mattress and the unaccustomed noise of six others in the room. There's dramatic moaning and groaning, overhead arm stretching and open-mouthed yawning. Everyone has to pass my bed as the shower and toilets are opposite. It didn't make for a quiet undisturbed night.

Breakfast is a pretty standard affair, with wheat-based cereals, tinned fruit, warm toast and jams. I meet Marjorie, she's in her late sixties, funny and entertaining, a quiet younger woman and a middle-aged man. My table mates for the day.

After breakfast we have housekeeping chores. Everyone takes part in cleaning the public spaces of the hospital and dorm duties before the first class. Chores are listed on the nurses station pin board and are changed daily, duties include sweeping and mopping floors, wiping window sills, washing dishes and cleaning the dorm showers and toilets. It brings some eye-rolling from the younger members of the groups but after dividing up the list we head off to the cleaning cupboard for brooms, mops and buckets, and toilet and shower cleaning products.

I use cleaning as a coping mechanism, a way to gain control from the chaos, washing everything I wear every day, stripping the bed, mopping floors, scrubbing the bathroom, cleaning cupboards. It's become compulsive, showering once or twice a day or when I feel dirty, not from anything physical but from the thoughts and feelings, the shame and humiliation that invade my mind from memories of the sexual abuse. When I'm upset, everything goes into the washing machine, sheets, what I'm wearing, towels, tea towels, everything I can lay my hands on. On truly bad days I see dirt and dust everywhere and the cleaning frenzy begins. I can feel my skin crawling and I have to strip off my clothes and begin again.

At our first class we meet the men who make up the other half of our group. The seven walk in and give us the same looks up and down that we're giving them. Again, they're mostly young and very cocky. We're a group of thirteen and while most of the work is co-ed, in sessions we will be separated.

All the chatter stops when an elderly man walks through the door. He's tall with bushy Santa eyebrows, heavy jowls, and thinning on top. He's wearing a long, well-worn green cardigan with small front pockets over a white shirt with navy trousers. He nods to us and walks across to the blackboard and writes in a beautiful cursive script *Father William*. The room remains silent.

This clearly wasn't what we were expecting, a priest not wearing a dog-collar, and into the silence Father William tells us his story. He's an alcoholic with fifteen years up. His evening glass of sherry escalated under stress until he needed a quick one before Sunday Services, church meetings, parish gatherings and visiting parishioners. His had a crisis of faith, stopped ministering and left the church. At this point he admitted he had a problem and joined Alcoholics Anonymous and then signed himself into rehab. In recovery, he's been reinstated into his church and in an act of giving back, gives his time teaching in the hospital program.

At the end of his story he stands before us, hands hidden in his cardigan pockets. For a minute or two no one speaks and then everyone begins to ask questions together. He answers questions about his faith, his belief in spirituality and God, his work as a local Catholic priest, hi work in the hospital with addict's. He tells us about working the 12-Steps and what we can expect if we take the Steps and the work in recovery seriously.

I'm trying to compare him to my memories of our family Methodist minister. I remember attending Sunday school with my sisters where we sat crossed legged on the floor in a side-room off the church. The minister's wife was in charge of the children's group and told us stories while holding up picture books, pointing to the baby Jesus surrounded by robed men, donkeys and lambs or riding a donkey while people waved long leafy branches. What I loved most was the weekly prayer card with the fancy gold writing and beautiful pictures of Mary in flowing robes, or God floating in clouds up in heaven with little fat babies, or Jesus walking with a tall stick, along a dusty road in sandals.

Mum was the religious one. She baptised her babies and expected her children to be married in a church. I don't remember either of my parents going to church or either of them being Methodists. However, as we had to walk and that was the closest church, that's the one we attended. My parents were very community minded and the annual church fair was one of their favourite events. Mum entered the jams and relishes competition and Dad entered the men's creamed sponge competition.

The final twenty minutes of our first class is spent having a general rant about what we don't like about Christianity, God, the church, the bible and priests. It seems no one has any positive memories about the church or the clergy, from judgemental attitudes through to hints of childhood sexual abuse. And while priests come in for some pretty angry outbursts, nuns don't fare any better. Overall, it's those children brought up in Catholic households who seem to hold the greatest grudges. The end of class is signal by the corridor bell and as we file out the noisy heated debate continues in the corridor.

4

The time-table directs us to the Theatre Room and when we enter the large space with the small stage at the far end, the overhead lighting, heavy red drapes and rows of chairs stacked against one wall, we understand how it got its name. At our end is a circle of fold-out chairs. The afternoon sun pours in through a bank of louvre windows, making the space extremely hot. We're here for our first *'Group'* session.

There's extra chairs so we expect others to join us. As if on cue, a number of staff enter and seat themselves randomly amongst us. The last person to arrive is a heavily bearded man, wheeling in an office chair with padded arms. He pushes the chair to the farthest end of the circle, facing the door, and placing the books he has under his arm on the floor, takes his seat.

This is Charles and he's the Group leader. He goes around the circle introducing the staff who nod or wave. We're told these sessions are daily and will take up the entire afternoon. Group makes up the core of all our recovery work, understanding the disease of addiction, uncovering the root cause of addiction, addressing behaviour, pinpointing problems with our thinking, the risks of relapse, changing self-beliefs and covering the first five steps in the Twelve Steps.

It all trips off Charles's tongue easily and sends my head into overdrive. It seems a long list to accomplish in four weeks when most of the words seem like jargon. Before I have time to process anything else Charles continues.

Group has rules. It's to be a safe space for all and any threatening behaviour, verbal or physical, means instant dismissal which is often called *on-the-bus*. Profanity is unacceptable. Leaving the room during a session is viewed as unacceptable. You may stand, approach the door, hold the door handle. But you are not allowed to walk through the door. The last rule is everyone must sit in a different place around the circle each day and beside someone new. The exception will be Charles himself, who will remain at the head of the circle in his padded arm office chair.

I'm not sure how the others are feeling but I feel a bit like a deer caught in head lights. Group feels intense and a little aggressive. Things are beginning to feel real and suddenly I'm not feeling so sure. Being under the scrutiny of Charles and the staff is making me sweat, bringing up the old feeling of guilt and shame. I feel triggered and cross my arms over my chest, drawing my legs up under my chair, trying to make myself small. I want to hide.

We go around the circle talking about why we're here and my immediate thought goes to my grandfather's sexual abuse and my father's angry outbursts. They terrified me and left me feeling hyper-alert whenever they were around. Then my mind jumps to the violent relationships, the years of battering, escaping and never really feeling safe. I sit with these weighing on my mind, shame and guilt rising like nausea and when it's my turn to speak, I say I had a happy childhood.

I give my edited version, just the general highlights. It's the story I've been telling for years, by rote, without thought, separate from who I really am and how I really feel. My parents are still together, I'm the eldest of eight children, mother of two boys. I didn't like school, got into trouble a lot, couldn't read, spell or do arithmetic. I was bullied in the playground for being fat, body-shamed and angry. I was pregnant at seventeen, married at eighteen and divorced at twenty three.

Everyone's story has a similar thread, despite the variety of backgrounds. Parents together or divorced. Some struggled at school, others didn't. A few lived in foster care, a couple were adopted. There's married, single, shacked up. Mothers, fathers and step-parents. There's a businessman, a guy who's just got out of jail and another who's been in and out all his life. A couple of the young women are prostitutes and want to escape that life.

When everyone's finished, we sit quietly and are startled when the counsellor called Chelsey begins to clap and cheer. She looks at each of us in turn, directing her clapping and cheering toward us and as we're not sure how to react, we go on sitting quietly.

"Well, Charles," she says, looking his way. "In the ten or more years I've been working here I've never heard such rubbish, have you? Lies, hot air, life's great and if there's any problems it's not my fault. Lots of blaming and finger pointing, lots of 'I'm the victim, I don't deserve this.'"

"They're rank amateurs," says Charles. "Okay people, we're going to break the habit of a lifetime and start telling the truth. Not only about what happened to you, but your part in it. How you felt at the time and how you feel now."

I lean straight-backed in my chair and stare up at the blinding light coming through the windows. I've told myself and others the truth about the sexual abuse for years. I was a child, I was coerced, I was a victim of an adult. What I never talk about is how I liked the attention. How I enjoyed being special. How I especially liked getting a chocolate teddy bear treat.

Soul Connection

Mum was always busy with the younger ones, she didn't have time for me. When she did call on me it was to bring in the washing, or set the table, or peel potatoes, or feed the cat. Of course, what my grandfather did hurt and I cried. But I shut out the pain of his poking fingers, disappeared into my head and told myself stories. He was the one who said, *"I love you and you're my special little girl."*

What would I say if I told the truth? My childhood was dominated by my father's moods, my mother's emotional absence, and my grandfather's sexual abuse. I was the eldest but felt like an only child. I wanted attention but what I received was negative, I was constantly told I talked too much, I was loud, and heavy-footed. I harboured a huge resentment against the foster babies my mother took so much trouble and time with. For years, I thought she did it out of Christian duty because they were the children of unmarried mothers, but later I realised she did it for the money.

How do I talk about being a teenage mother? How do I reveal my stupidity and humiliation, my naivety and lack of social awareness? I can't, it's too humiliating, I thought I was behaving like a grown up, an adult, when really I was nothing but a silly child. I imagined myself to be responsible, reliable, and a good mother and friend, when really I was the opposite of all those things. I hate myself and have so much self-loathing. I feel worthless and unlovable, I've made a mess of my life, and my children's lives, and I don't know how to fix it. I don't know where to start. I'm so disgusted with myself.

I come back to the room and realise we're finished. Everyone is standing up, we're being pulled into a circle, closer, arms around each other's waists. Head bowed, Father William leads us in the Serenity Prayer.

God grant me the serenity to accept the things I cannot change.
Courage to change the things I can
And wisdom to know the difference.

5

It's on the schedule, part of the program, and while they say it's not compulsory, really it is. Every evening after dinner, the entire hospital, staff and patients, walk down to the village to attend either the Alcoholics Anonymous or Narcotics Anonymous Meeting. It's a pleasant walk across the hospital grounds, out the side gate, and past the closed tourist shops, their windows full of lambskin goods for the bus loads of local tourists and overseas travellers.

We file into the village hall and wander over to the small crowd gathered around the supper table. There's hot drinks and plates of plain biscuits. Chairs have been set out, A.A. and Twelve Step banners hung and a wooden podium with an adjustable microphone on the stage. In dribs and drabs we take our seats.

I don't like being in the middle of a crowd so usually choose to sit down the front. It's also easier to get up when we're asked to '*share*'. We're encouraged to share at every Meeting, especially when we're just starting our recovery. I do find it helps to hear the stories of those who've got sober '*time up*' and learn how their lives have changed. It's what we all want; change.

Sometimes it can be hard, hearing old war stories about rape, sexual abuse or violence against wives or girlfriends. Or listening to women talking about domestic abuse or date rape. There are good stories, parents united with their estranged children and family, rekindling of relationships or marriage after years of destructive drinking or using. My favourite stories are about those who've found a spiritual path, especially after homelessness, mental health issues or unemployment.

I want to believe these things are possible when you're sober. I want to find my children and repair the damage I've done to them and their lives. I want the chance to explain myself to my parents, my family and friends. I want to be a different person, to have a job, a home, a supportive network. I hang on every word of those who have managed their first year or five, not because I don't think I'll be sober in one or five years, but to learn how they got their life back, how they found happiness and escaped the misery that's my life at present.

In all the years I was drinking and using drugs it never occurred to me to stop. I didn't think about it or consider it. Not even when my social using became an all day, every day habit. I either ignored, dismissed or worked around the problems of being in *black out*, of not being able to care for my sons or managing the household. I lived in a world of high drama, anxiety, conflict, antisocial conduct and unreasonable behaviour. I just poured myself another glass of wine or rolled another joint and let life either revolve around me or, most of the time, run right over me.

It didn't think I was doing anything wrong or that it was affecting me or having an adverse effect on my children or their lives. It became normal, just how it was, and I saw no reason to examine or change it. Life was a survival skill, bouncing from one problem to the next and continually hitting that unseen wall. I never thought about the walls, why they kept happening or figured out how to stop them. I simply turned away and got hit by the unexpected arrival of the next.

Speaker after speaker walks up, adjusts the microphone and tells their story. Some share a problem they're having, others a win or an insight, a change of behaviour that suddenly makes sense and everything falls into place. I make my story quick, just sharing how it feels to be in the hospital working the program. I don't linger at the microphone, anxious to get back to my seat.

We're invited to stay and talk, meet the locals and share another cup of tea and biscuit but the hospital has its own supper routine with a sing-along, so we head back. On the walk home it's mostly a reflective mood with little or no talk. But I can't let go of the belief that in every circumstance I've been the victim, oppressed, exploited and having no power. But is that true? There's been times when I've bullied, taken advantage, manipulated, lied, cheated and used emotional blackmail to get what I've wanted. That makes me an abuser too.

I feel this split, the victim and the perpetrator. Half of me is self-righteous, ready to blame others and point the finger. While knowing I've also caused harm, done damage and been irresponsible and negligent. The warring factions are screaming in my head, a ping pong game, each pleading their case, defending their actions, accusing and blaming.

When I get back to the hospital I go straight to the dorm. I don't want to join in the singing, I need to scribble down what's going on in my head, try to make sense of my thoughts. Can I be both a victim of others and a person who mistreats others verbally and emotionally?

THE WEEKEND

Insanity is defined as doing the same thing over and over again, while expecting different results.

6

I wake to a sleeping dorm. I stretch out my legs and wriggle my toes. It's Saturday with no classes, no Group, just the luxury of time. That's the most difficult thing about the program so far, never having enough time to digest or process anything. The pressure never lets up, rushing from class to class, from this therapy session to the next, being talked to by yet another health professional.

Group is brutal. It's like fighting a multi-headed monster coming at you from all corners of the room, challenging everything you say, every word you speak, every behaviour, every action, with no wriggle space. Being pushed to tell the truth and face reality. To be upfront, honest, and talk about your emotions and how you feel. The comfort of lies, half-truths, pretence and denial gone. The emotional vulnerability of parading naked down the street while everyone gets to judge your body.

And the dreaded *'Hot Seat'*. Just you, separated from the group, while the counsellors and therapists pick, pick, pick. Examining your attitudes, beliefs, negativity, judgmentalism and analysing your internal self-talk.

Testing your thinking, does it stand up to the reality test? Reviewing what you've said, is it an all or nothing view, black or white reasoning, positive or negative, are you falling into *stinking thinking*...?

Living with five dramatic, over the top, highly sensitive young women who periodically fight, argue and scream is reminding me of my girls-only High School years. Most of the time everyone makes an effort to get along but sometimes the tension builds and it feels as if the roof will be blown off.

It's been an eventful and emotionally charged first week and although it's only been five days it feels more like five months. My head feels like it's been in a continue wash cycle. I throw off the blankets and hurrying, pull on my clothes, grab my journal and head outside. I need some me time.

WEEK TWO

One Day at a Time.

7

I get it. We're addicts. We thrive on drama, theatrics, rushing from one calamity to the next, catastrophizing life and making every striking match into a towering inferno. Our lives are one long soap opera with a new tragedy every day, running on adrenaline, stress, anxiety and continual chaos.

To maintain sobriety we need to slow down, stay calm, stop the drama and end the chaos. To find balance we need to embrace stability and normality. This is the reason we're in the hospital and working the program, to get some structure into our lives. A routine of getting up and getting dressed, cleaning the space around us, having three meals a day, regular exercise and counselling. A bell to wake up and a curfew at night. Making beds, attending classes, seeing counsellors and going to Alcoholics Anonymous Meetings.

My mind feels sharper. More of us are taking part in the discussions and not just giving monosyllabic answers. My general concentration is improving, I'm less argumentative, slower to anger, not so much defensiveness, less sensitive or prickly. They're still pushing our buttons in Group and getting under people's skin but we're not so reactive.

It's noticeable that some of the younger men are shaving more often and their clothes look tidier. There's more lipstick being used and some of the women are doing each other's hair. The pink hair dryer is getting a workout. While there's still discarded clothing strewn on the dorm floor, the magazines and make up is being tidied away. There's less acting out, less huffing and puffing, the habits of others isn't causing the same conflict. Things are calming down.

After a long and boring weekend everyone is pleased to be back in class. There were too many hours to fill without the excitement of a party, getting drunk, causing a fight, having an argument and being tossed out of a club by the bouncer. We'd played charades, cards, board games, Pictionary and watched videos till it felt like our eyes would bleed.

On the blackboard is the word '*Thinking*'. There's the routine grizzle as we take our seats. Father William stands at the front of the class, hands in pockets, his usual enigmatic smile on his face.

I'm not the only one who thought getting sober meant saying no to alcohol and drugs. I had no idea what a major role thinking played in our addition. I suppose as an addict you stop being aware of what you're thinking. It's background noise to using, everything just becomes a habit, ritualistic behaviour, your favourite wine glass, beer mug, dope tin, smoking device. The ceremony of preparation, opening the wine, rolling the joint, taking that first sip, that first deeply-held breath. What we're learning is that below the habit is the thinking, the thoughts that fuel our addiction. The negative and persistent thinking that drives our desire to always return to drinking and drug use.

Father William, chalk in hand, stands ready for suggestions of our negative thinking. There's a long list: I hate my parents, life isn't fair, why me, nobody cares, my mother didn't love me, I hated school, my parents divorced when I was ten. There's also racial slurs and sexist comments that Father William refuses to write on the board.

What he does write on the board is that we can change our thinking!

I struggle with this idea. I thought how we felt or what we thought were set in concrete. That at some point we came up with how we thought about something, like I hate the colour blue, and it stayed like that for life. I find I have a long list in my head. But as I sit and mull this over I realise a lot of the things I don't like I'm actually frightened of. I'm quite fearful of many of the things that are everyday life. Maybe I'm not very trusting. These thoughts bring up a sense of panic and I find I have to take a couple of breaths and slow my breathing.

I put my hand up and say, "I hate blue. I always have and always will."

I tell the class about being dressed in blue as a child while my younger sisters wore pinks and lemon, pretty shades of green and sometimes white with lace or ribbons. Mum made our clothes and often dressed us in the same style, in four different colours. I was always dressed in blue.

Even now I can feel how I felt as a child; lumpy and fat, unattractive with a big nose and unruly curly hair. The unlovable little girl who was excited about wearing her new dress to school until the other girls made fun of me. I wasn't *girly* like my sisters. I was useless at sport. I couldn't run or jump and wasn't picked to be on any team. I was always at the bottom of the class, getting the strap for being lazy and not doing my homework, or being disruptive and talking too much.

Father William points out I associate all those feelings with the colour blue. That I blamed blue for my childhood suffering. I'm struck dumb. My mind is whirling. In a single sentence Father William has reorganised my childhood thinking and I'm left sitting in a puddle of mixed emotions.

I need time to think this through and get a better understanding. I can already sense the feelings dropping away from the sad schoolgirl I see in my mind. All those childhood embarrassments, the shame and feelings of self-hatred are suddenly, clearly, no longer part of the colour blue. But they're also painful and I feel rejected and friendless and unloved. I stand alone in the school grounds, abandoned and unacceptable. And the colour blue has nothing to do with how I feel.

8

I'm sitting on a bench under the trees trying to write in my journal but I'm being distracted by the smell of freshly cut grass. It takes me back to memories of dad mowing the lawn after work, walking up and down, leaving bright green stripes behind him.

But that's not what I came out here to write about. I can't get Billy's story from Group out of my mind. It was gut-wrenching. Not just the feelings his story brought up but also the off-handed way he told it. In all the years he was in foster care he never had a birthday party.

We had parties when we were at school. All the neighbourhood kids were invited and a couple of special friends from our class. There were sandwiches with hundreds and thousands, peanut brownies, pink marshmallow slice, jelly and store-bought ice cream and a decorated birthday cake with a paper frill and coloured candles.

It made me sad and angry, and it hurt when he passed it off like a joke, making fun and pretending he didn't care. I might have been unhappy and felt alone but I always had my family and we always celebrated birthdays.

I watch myself drawing birthday cakes with tiny flaming candles, scribbling words around them, how it feels to know someone didn't have a childhood, wasn't celebrated, was cared about enough to make a special day of his birthday. I go from anger to tears, as feelings of being unwanted, unloved and forgotten well up inside.

Out of this misery comes my great idea. We'll give him a surprise party! My head is suddenly full of blowing up balloons, wrapping presents, lighting candles, singing *Happy Birthday*. I need to get everyone on board. Slamming my journal closed, I rush back to the dorm to find everyone.

It's fun decorating the room in secret, pinning up streamers and balloons. Decorating the table, making a pile of wrapped gifts and kiddie birthday cards. There's Disney paper plates, paper cups and colourful plastic cutlery. To top it all off, a fancy ice cream cake hidden in the kitchen fridge. We're giggling and saying how surprised Billy's going to be, telling stories of our worst birthday presents and what we wished for when blowing out the candles.

My fondest memory is mum's famous jelly rabbit. I'll always remember the yellow plastic rabbit mould and filling it upside down with the boiling water jelly mix and walking it carefully to the fridge to set. We'd stand at the kitchen bench, fingers crossed, and scream with delight when the undamaged rabbit sat wobbling on its plate of chopped green-jelly grass. At the table there be arguments as to who got the nose, the ears, the fat round cottontail.

At last everything is ready and one of the men is sent to fetch Billy while we duck behind the table, the curtains or squeeze behind the door. We wait so long I get pins and needles in my toes and have to wriggle them to make the blood flow. At last we hear the men talking and get ready to leap out. We're slightly hysterical by the time the door opens and we jump up shouting, "Surprise!"

Billy is genuinely surprised and we are so pleased with ourselves there's congratulations, hugging, slapping each other on the back and general chaos. Billy stands just inside the door, gazing around at the coloured streamers and the bouncing balloons. He seems speechless when he finally walks around the table, reaching out but not quite touching the spread of chips and dips, the iced cup-cakes and chocolate biscuits, the bowls of jelly beans and party mix. The bottles of coke and orange juice. We keep watching Billy's face, delighting in his wide eyes and inability to respond to all we've done.

It's all very silly and lots of fun. We fill our paper plates and take our drinks to sit on one of the plastic chairs we've place around the edge of the room. There's lots of noise and cross chatter, everyone is talking at once, it's as if we haven't seen each other in months and are trying to catch up in five minutes. It feels like the last barrier to feeling safe with each other is gone and we're willing to finally relax in each other's company, to be friends.

It's time to open the presents. Billy takes his time, becoming very earnest, slowly pulling the tape off and then diligently unwrapping the paper. There's a packet of grey plastic soldiers and the guys immediately fall on them and set up rival army camps, making pretend firing noises.

It's the same slow production with the next present and at last a colourful spinning top falls into Billy's large, meaty hand. The soldiers are forgotten and it's a competition to see who can make the top spin the longest. There's a watch timer involved.

There's a bright red tractor wooden puzzle, a kite-making kit and a dress-up cowboy outfit with a holster and plastic gun. Billy pins the sheriff badge on his shirt and does a hoedown dance waving his new cowboy hat in a circle around his head.

I slip out and fetch the cake, lighting the candles before slipping through the door. With a nod, someone turns the lights off and we all sing *Happy Birthday* at the top of our lungs. I choke up seeing everyone gathered around the table, around Billy. I feel I've returned a lost part of his childhood to him, filled a hole, healed a wound he was carrying.

In the moment I'm connected to something outside of myself and also in touch with something inside. I'm encouraged and positive that we as a group can make it. We can overcome our childhood trauma, our addiction and past mistakes. We can remake ourselves and become better people. I'm content to retreat to the corner and watch our childish party flow around me. We're all happy, smiling and having fun. Tomorrow, it'll be back to work but for now we're proud of ourselves.

9

It's late afternoon and we're sluggish, tired and irritable. Group was gruelling and the sight of afternoon tea laid out on the rose garden steps is a welcome sight. Maybe the afternoon will be easier after a biscuit, a hot drink and fifteen minutes sitting in the sun. But that's not to be. When we enter the classroom there's a stranger wearing a black suit with dog collar and silver cross pinned to his lapel. There's also a Bible on each desk.

It's a shock to find ourselves in a religious class. We're so used to thinking of Father William as the Christian representative on staff that the idea of being preached to by someone else causes a universal groan. If we were expecting the understanding, empathic wisdom of Father William we are soon disabused of that idea. This priest is more the fire and brimstone ilk. He stands at the front of the class, his gold-edged Bible open in hand, reading passage after passage, ready to forgive our sins if we turn our lives over to Christ.

Mum would love this. She's been trying to drag me back to the Church and make a good Christian of me for years. And she hasn't been subtle about it. There was the time a minister just happened to be passing and popped in for a chat about what the Bible had to say about divorce. That was after running around town trying to find one of the local churches who was prepared to officiate at a shot-gun wedding. Then there was the long letter when I came out, urging me to beg for God's forgiveness and give my life over to Jesus. She also absolved herself of any responsibility for my turning out to be a deviant.

The curious thing about mum, she was also a very sensitive, intuitive woman. She felt the presence of spirits, saw ghosts, intuitively knew when the postman left mail, could put a name to the person on the phone before picking up the receiver, and had beds made up before visitors arrived. She was practical, realistic, organised and in every way a down to earth woman. She believed in the stories about fairies and elves, took note of her dreams, but was also fearfully superstitious.

She wouldn't have Arum lilies in the house; they foretold a death, but she grew them by the dozen in the garden. She wore a rabbit foot brooch for luck, didn't believe black cats were unlucky, guarded against breaking mirrors or walking under ladders and believed good or bad luck came in threes.

One of the things I'm most grateful for was allowing me to grow up with no fear of my intuition, relating to spirits, and seeing the dead. At fourteen my grandmother came and stood at the end of my bed the day before her funeral, my father did the same. Because of my mother I've never been frightened or concerned by any supernatural experience. However, I never told her about my *quiet whispering voice*. I'm not sure why.

It wasn't frightening, it didn't alarm me, it was calm and reassuring, whispering things that were going to happen, something someone said or was going to say to me or do. The voice was female and it felt like living with perpetual deja vu.

In the six months since I've stopped drinking and using drugs I've begun to feel Her presence more strongly, more like when I was a child. The quieter my head becomes, the less obsessional my thoughts, the more clearly I hear Her voice. As I understood the A.A. message of a Higher Power the more I turn to Her whispering message. This is a true connection with my Inner Self, my Wiser Self.

I snap back to the class and realise the readings have stopped, the Bible is closed and people are leaving. I've no idea what's been said but I have an hour before the dinner bell to catch up on my journal writing.

10

It feels like I've been wandering around in circles for hours and even with the directions I can't find the counsellor's office. Most of the hospital counsellors are staff members who turn up at Group or a classroom. However, this morning my appointment is with an independent practitioner and she shares a private office somewhere behind the back entrance. It's a little prefab tucked away at the back of the gardening sheds. When I knock on the door it's opened by a rosy-cheeked woman about my age, who invites me in and points to the larger of two chairs in front of an untidy desk.

I haven't been in many counsellors rooms but they seem to have a common theme of inspirational words for clients to stare at, something smelly wafting around the room and vases of flowers or dishes of crystals or sea shells. Plus the dozens of book-lined wooden shelving.

Alice is friendly, inviting and easy to talk to. She has me feeling relaxed in no time. We chat, I tell her more about myself and how things are going in the hospital, with the group and the program and I guess that's how it's supposed to be. After all that's what I'm here for, to talk about myself. She's taking notes in the pad resting on her knee.

Just when I think everything is going well the conversation falters. Alice doesn't seem to know what to say next. She's distracted, shifts in her seat, recrossing her legs and toying with her pen. When she looks out the window I turn to see what she's looking at, but there's only the garden sheds and blue sky.

Her nervousness is making me nervous and whereas moments ago I was feeling trusting, now I'm trying to figure out what's going on. Her question, when she asks, is so unexpected for a moment I don't know how to answer. It's not that I'm reluctant to answer, just the subject hasn't come up in other counselling sessions or Group. She wants to know how I knew I was a lesbian.

I have to stop and think, it seems such a long time ago. I must have been in my late twenties. I think I've forgotten about the years I was heterosexual, the marriage, the birth of my children, finding feminism and *'Coming Out'*.

It occurs to me Alice might be struggling with her own identity and has questions about Coming Out. I imagine it's just as hard being in the health profession, and a small community, as any other. I stop and wonder if this is going to turn into one of those sessions where I counsel the counsellor. It's happened before. While everyone loves having a gay person they feel comfortable to ask questions, in this situation it's my health and welfare that should be the priority.

There's no point being evasive so I ask her directly if that's the reason for the question and it is. She has all the same problems me or anyone else has, who to tell, what to say, when's the best time, what will people think, will they judge her, turn their backs, will she lose her job? I sympathise, we've all been in this situation and while it's different for everyone, it's also the same.

It's especially difficult if you don't know any lesbians to talk with. Alice isn't sure she can talk to friends or colleges, and she's not ready to talk to any of the hospital staff, given the administration's history of homophobia. There was talk in A.A. about mandatory rules about women wearing 'appropriate feminine clothing', no pants or trousers, no boots and women were also expected to wear some makeup. Men were also targeted for being *effeminate*. For a number of years it hadn't been considered safe for lesbians or gay men to be admitted to the hospital for substance abuse treatment.

Alice wants to use her upcoming significant birthday to tell friends and family. But the closer it gets the more she's frightened of the consequences. It's very isolating in a small town. I suggest she contact a support group in the city and start working on a support network.

To break the tension I tell her a funny story about a friend trying to tell me I was a lesbian. I had crushes on straight friends and this particular friend thought she'd help. All I remember of the conversation was that she had an aunt who liked women and had moved to Australia so as not to cause her family any pain. I didn't recognise myself in the story and I left as ignorant of my sexuality as when I arrived. Years later, when it finally dawned on me what she'd been trying to tell me, I laughed and laughed.

Alice has her own stories and it's very pleasant sitting in the cosy intimacy of her office without thinking about what's happening outside. It's a break from the constant examination of our life, the mistakes and consequences of bad choices we've made. The constant harping on about our commitment to ourselves, our recovery, and what we're prepared to do for long term sobriety.

It feels like a proper girls talk with someone my age and my sexuality. It's always different talking with one of your own. I haven't hidden my sexuality but I also haven't brought it up in general conversation. I'm not here as a lesbian, I'm here as an addict and I don't want the focus to shift. I made one decision when I applied; if my addiction was blamed on my being a lesbian I was prepared to leave.

We're happy to sit around and gossip, rehash crushes, tell stories of our first love. I was a teenager working at an after school job in our local hair salon when I fell madly in love with one of the senior hairdressers. I ran around helping and doing errands, fetching her lunch, picking up her dry cleaning. I don't remember feeling anything sexual but I did think I was acting like a man. When she got engaged I cried for a week.

It's hard to go back and try to remember what your thinking was at the time. I know I had very emotional friendships with women but still thought if I wanted sex it would be with a man. Some of these intense female friendships lasted for years and were very emotionally satisfying, unlike the sexual relationships I had with men. It wasn't until I joined the feminist movement and met lesbians that I began to understood it was possible to have a deeply emotional and sexual relationships with women.

There's a knock on the door and Alice is confronted by a concerned nurse looking for me. It seems we've been talking for hours and the staff have sent out a search party.

11

No one wants to be first and nor do I. I'm happy to stand in a circle around the pile of old telephone books, pages ripped and torn, yellow covers in tatters or missing, and contemplate how they got that way. I suspect the answer lies with Belinda; she's facilitating this afternoon's exercise, and is cradling a wooden baseball bat in her arms. It's simple enough, take the bat and hit the books. It's an anger exercise.

Anger is something addicts have in great measure. Apparently we need to find appropriate ways to release our anger and beating up a pile of old telephone books is one of those ways. My experience of anger left me feeling distrustful of my father, adults in general and the world. My own rage has caused a variety of problems, from screaming in an out of control outburst when bumped while drinking at the bar, to losing my temper at my children or friends or strangers, when I was highly stressed or couldn't get the results I wanted.

My anger frightens, it feels so out of control, but anger in others also feels frightening and out of control. I don't react well to being challenged, I usually retaliate inappropriately, or if I need to sort out a problem I either become loud and act like a bully, or submit and become the victim. I don't know how to respond suitably and tend to get big and huffy, believing yelling will get me what I want, which is not to be questioned. Or I get all wimpy and lie, or say whatever I think they want to hear and hate myself later.

Today's exercise comes after a long session in Group about resentments and holding onto them. Being bitter and angry, holding a grudge, never letting go of the cruel words and deeds done to us are the poison that can fuel our addiction. Wanting revenge, obsessing about payback, sharing evidence to get others to confirm you're *right* and they are *wrong* leads to more resentment, more bitterness and more anger and rage.

Forgiveness is being suggested as the answer. Changing our thinking, thought redirection, dealing with the underlying emotions and letting go of the unhappy and bitter feelings associated with our thoughts is all part of forgiveness. But first we need to deal with those suppressed emotions and get the anger out.

The hall seems very large and empty around our small circle. It's just us girls today and Belinda, holding out the bat handle, assures us no one will hear, the hall is ours until we're done. But that isn't making us any less nervous about grabbing the bat and beating the shit out of a pile of old books. It's an act of such vulnerability and no one, especially me, is prepared to step up.

What happens when I get in touch with all those feelings, the resentment, rage, sadness, grief, regret, heart ache, sorrow, what then? When it's all been spewed out, what happens then? Where would it go, could I ever pack it away again or live without it? It's been sitting in my belly for so long it's almost a familiar comfort. I'm panicking at the thought of giving it up, not having it to make me feel alive. Sometimes I think it's the only thing keeping me connected to myself.

It's bad enough dealing with these new feelings; being sober is like being an all-seeing, all-hearing, all-knowing being, like being naked and feeling the slightest breeze and reacting to the slightest wind change. Where once I felt nothing, now I feel everything. There's no hiding, no time out. I don't believe I can deal with that amount of emotional overload by simply beating on a pile of paper.

I watch the others, marvelling at their ability to beat the books, to swing the bat again and again, until their faces are red and dripping with sweat. Pieces of the books fly into the air and across the floor. Belinda chases after them, picking them up and throwing them back on the pile. We join in, flinging books, singing out, stomping our feet and clapping our hands. Soon it's not scary or intimidating, it's thrilling.

I swoop in and grab the bat before it's dropped on the floor. I feel its weight as I throw it up and onto my shoulder and start bringing it down. It slams down, giving a little bounce. It feels good. The physical power, feet planted apart, arms taking the weight, the bat smashing into the books. I become lost inside, on autopilot, unaware of my surroundings.

I'm back in my grandfather's house watching my father leave the room and close the door. I know he's across the hall in the kitchen, talking to Nana. They're making a cup of tea and eating slices of bread and butter with jam. They'll be a long time, talking. While I'm alone with my grandfather and his beckoning finger. As I stand in front of him, I stare as his long fleshy ears with their grey spouting hairs.

The image in my head morphs into scene after scene of my father's anger, him looming, stomping up the back stairs and charging into the house. His bellowing through the bedroom wall for my sister and I to *"Shut up!"* and go to sleep. My mother's tears when she grabbed the steering wheel to go back home for my two little sisters, left behind because they disobeyed him.

Soul Connection

Feeling the rising fear when I know my partner is baiting and bullying me, trying to find an excuse to take out her frustration on me. Working herself to fever pitch so she can let go of reason and just kick and punch and let off steam.

All the times I've been called fatty, wolf whistled from a building site, told I wasn't acting like a lady, keep your legs together and don't show your knickers. Every snide, look-down-their-nose, cruel, woman-hating comment. The shame of being yelled at and called a fag, dyke, fairy, homo, sicko. All the times I was frightened, unsure, anxious, and felt hate, shame and humiliation, is flowing out of my body through the end of the bat as it smashes the paper, the pages, the books.

When I finally come back to myself I'm sitting on the floor, tears pouring down my face with someone asking if I'm alright. It's like coming out of a waking dream, a nightmare. I'm not sure where I am or who the women are standing around me. I feel around me for the bat, my wooden sword, but it's gone. I pull my knees up and cover my head with my arms. It's too soon to come back to the room, to the women. I'm not ready to acknowledge the depth of my rage, to admit how much anger I've stored up, carried around, suppressed and pretended didn't exist. It's been my defence, keeping people at bay, a wall of negative energy saying, "Stay back, stay away."

My head is pounding as we leave the hall, my arms aching as if I've done a heavy workout at the gym. But my spirit feels light, as if I've removed a set of unacknowledged amour, a weight off my shoulders. I feel like skipping, like that little girl before she lost her childhood innocence, prey to her grandfather's sexual gratification.

12

I take off my shoes and leave them at the door, adding to the line. I pull a rolled yoga mat from the cupboard and find a place on the floor under the windows. The blinds are down but there's a gap of escaping sunlight that shines on my face. As the last people settle, a hush falls over the room. It's Father William's belief that the breath is prayer and while he calls this class an hour of spiritual devotion, I think of it as sixty minutes of heavenly silence. Although sharing is allowed if you're so moved.

The intense pleasure of just letting my body sink into the slab of foam. To let my limbs become weightless, eyes closed, aware of all those around me and yet not aware. To join the breath in and out of my neighbours and let the worries of the day drift away. To focused on the nothingness in my mind, to watch my thoughts rushing by and yet not to be taken away from the stillness.

The wall. I'm obsessed by the wall. An imaginary coping mechanism devised to keep my Inner Self safe. A wall that gives my Inner Child somewhere to hide. Behind the wall I've stored my secrets, my desires, who I really am. Meanwhile on the outside I've become defensive, shut down emotionally, ready to fight back, remaining always alert and ready for danger.

I often draw the wall in my journal. I use a red pen and make the bricks even and straight. I draw a funny stick figure of the child on one side and the armed warrior on the other. Behind the endless rows of bricks I feel secure and protected. I go there, in my head, when I feel overwhelmed and unable to cope with my out world life.

I don't remember a time when the wall wasn't there. A brick was added, one at a time for every hurt, wound, broken promise, verbal attack, bruise, broken bone, shattered guarantee or coercive argument. Built to keep my damaged, distrustful child-self safe from more pain, sadness, emotional and physical damage. A barrier between me and the world.

But now I'm discovering the wall has become a fortress that keeps me from sharing my emotions, from being able to express my feelings. What was once safety is now a prison keeping my heart hostage and I'm frightened I won't find the key. While on the outside I don't know how to take off the layers of protection, I've become so defensive, wary and uncaring.

In a horrible irony, the barrier I've created to keep myself safe is the barrier between me and my sons, making it almost impossible for me to show them anything but my irresponsibility and selfishness as their mother. The wall has distanced me from my family and friends, and stopped me from being able to reach out for the help and support I need.

But hiding behind the wall, and being in denial, hasn't made me feel any braver or less afraid. It hasn't given me the time or space to become more confident, sociable, friendly or outgoing. It's only increased my fears and made me more timorous and apprehensive. I'm still that frightened little girl hiding in the shadows, intimidated by bullies, terrified of authority figures and fearful of making decisions, knowing my every choice will be wrong.

I'm still a victim of those who are dominating and who wield power through coerce and control. If I'm to make the most of my time in rehab, in recovery, I have to be willing to dismantle the wall, possibly one brick at a time.

I've come full circle. The wall that was once my safety holds me in incarceration, the alcohol and drugs that once made life easy and manageable are now the jailers holding the keys. If I'm to take back control of my life I need a new foundation, not the bricks of negativity and brokenness but the bricks of truth and honesty. From the far side of the room I hear Father William's voice as he leads the Serenity Prayer.

Courage to change the things I can . . .

THE WEEKEND

Formula for failure – Try to please everyone.

13

I have my own room. Just me and my clothes and books and Maude the bear. It's wonderful, no mindless chatter, no hair dryers, no wandering youngsters in various states of undress, no wafting cigarette smoke or cheap perfume, no bags, shoes or discarded clothing to trip over. Just the silence of living on my own, in tranquillity and peace.

It's like a nun's cell, a simple single bed, a bedside chest under the window and a small wardrobe crouching at the end of the room. The walls are bare and the roller blind doesn't work. I don't care, it's all mine.

I lie in the luxury of silence and time. I stretch my legs and wiggle my toes. I want to rush outside to the new day and I also want to stay in bed and be lazy. We're halfway through and most of the time I'm managing to cope and the rest of the time my mind is mush. The hospital has become home, I know the staff, enjoy the routine and understand what the program is trying to provide. I'm not as sensitive or super self-protective and while I still find Group painful and upsetting, I'm more willing to push beyond what's comfortable and try to stay real and honest.

Soul Connection

I know my thinking has changed. The judgemental black and white attitude is dropping away and I'm seeing more sides to every issue. I'm prepared to listen rather than jump in with my opinion, my story, my experience or how I think it should be done. I'm learning empathy for myself and for others. My conscience is developing and rather than make excuses or ducking responsibility by telling lies or looking for others to blame, I'm owning up.

At times I find it hard to concentrate. My mind is sluggish and it's easy to drift off and escape into my imagination. I still have times of not being able to focus even though I haven't used alcohol or drugs for over six months. My brain feels like a mill stone, resistant and unmovable. It takes all my will power and concentration to push through to the answers I know are stored there. I'm learning the art of self-examination and self-reflection, to uncover my part in the action I took and what motivated me.

I wonder how long it will take to undo the damage I've done to my brain and mind through twenty-odd years of alcohol and drug abuse.

WEEK THREE

Surrender to become Victorious.

14

Father William writes two words on the blackboard, *Religion* and *Spirituality*, sparking an immediate reaction from the class. All week we've been talking about a spiritual base to our recovery, a Higher Power, a God as we understood Him. It's a difficult concept to embrace for those who have been turned off or let down by the church, clergy, Christianity, Jesus or God. However, turning your life over to your Higher Power is the very fundamental message of the Twelve Steps. Addiction is a spiritual breakdown.

We hear first Father William's story of organised religion and his experience as a Catholic priest. He talks about religion as a specific set of beliefs and practices, shared by the Christian community. He gives his views on Christianity, the church, Christian faith, beliefs, dogma and practices. He touches on the life of Jesus Christ. He ends with the question of who has read the Bible?

I haven't read the Bible but have heard much of its writing quoted as a reason to single out gay people to be sinners and unacceptable within most Christian based churches. There's plenty of stories about trauma and abuse from the priesthood, clergymen and nuns, verbal, physical and sexual. We all know of situations where scripture was used as a weapon to defend judgmental abuse, racism and homophobia.

Father William doesn't defend the church or its teachings. He stands quietly, hands in his cardigan pockets, listening to our examples of ill treatment, anger or shame, at the hands of a Christian school, Sunday school or church. He doesn't justify, make excuses or retaliate. He quietly continues talking about his view of spirituality.

Unlike an external experience, he sees spirituality as a personal, internal experience, a connection with your Inner Self. A way to find meaning in your life, a way to connect the inner life with the life force of nature all around us. A belief system that springs from an intention to live within your personal understanding, answering the question of "How should I live?"

I'm comfortable with spirituality. I accepted hearing a Voice in my head when I was a child. It was always female and at odds with what I was being taught in Sunday School. God was something outside and I heard the Voice inside. God was frightening and so many things about the Bible and Jesus didn't make sense to me. I loved the stories but found them hard to believe. I tested the all-seeing, all-knowing God by telling a couple of whoppers and nothing happened. The quiet, whispering Voice comforted and reassured me. She made me felt safe. She warned me with words and feelings in my stomach.

I've used my journal for years to connect with my Inner Self. Journaling is a form of meditation and reflection. I began each day scribbling, writing down all those thoughts that circle in my mind, disturbing my peace. Pushing past the grocery list, ringing the plumber, letting the cat in, until I'm connected and communicating with my Inner Voice, my Authentic Self.

The more my mind clears, the stronger I'm finding that Inner Voice which I don't find surprising as I've heard stories from A.A. members about the spiritual experiences in rehab. Happenings and events that made sense at the time, chance encounters that led to powerful insights or random acts of kindness that changed racist or homophobic attitudes. Finding the right book, the right page, the right sentence that makes everything suddenly fall into place. The light bulb moments without rational explanation that become that fateful coincidence of transformation, the insight that changes a point of view, the idea that takes a floundering person and puts them back on their feet.

This spiritual experience, we're told, is a necessary part of our recovery. Without a connection to a power greater than ourselves we'll never maintain sobriety. Willpower alone isn't going to solve the problem of our addiction. It requires surrender, an attitude of acceptance and giving up the illusion of control. That, declares Father William, is why we're asked to hand our lives over to our Higher Power and to give our life new meaning.

It's challenging for resentful, bitter, self-centred, negative thinking addicts to accept a new set of principles to live by. To let go the old ideas of blame, resentfulness and self-righteousness. But that's exactly what we need to do. Acceptance and handing over our life, without the need to fix or control. To stop worrying, overthinking and pre-empting events with a hundred what-if's. Being open to a spiritual life, Father William says, will fill the empty void inside and support a new connection with the world around us. He writes, *Let go and let God*, on the blackboard.

I remember being attracted to feminism, not because of the childhood sexual abuse or growing up with a misogynist father but because it gave me a more rational explanation about why the world was the way it was. I'd felt the effects of not being the boy my father wanted. And I soon understood what it meant not to meet the required standards of beauty for females. I felt the slurs of being a lesser person than men and saw how my father treated my mother, her tears and being shut down emotionally.

I found feminism to be a fit. It didn't take me long to become an advocate and militant activist. Feminism became my world, politically, spiritually, emotionally and sexually. I was an ardent believer in the social, economic, and political equality of the sexes. I read books, went to meetings, studied Herstory and found the Goddess, Paganism, witchcraft and Wicca.

Father William shares his spiritual awakening after losing his way and tells us about this personal experience during his recovery. A deeper connection to spirituality and a new connection with his God. I'm inspired by his story. I visualise a pair of cupped hands and I internally hand over all my worries and concerns. I grasp the belief that I will find my sons, I will repair the damage done to my children. I can become a new and responsible parent.

Father William's final words, written in his beautiful cursive script. . .

We came to believe that a power greater than ourselves could restore us to sanity.

15

I don't mind being the butt of the joke, the reason everyone is laughing. They're right, as the oldest it's bound to take me longer to write my *'moral inventory'*. It will probably be a book rather than a few pages and in keeping with the joke, everyone throws me a pen.

The laughter breaks the tension of Group where we've been discussing the writing of our Fourth Step, called by some, the confessional. This is where we list the secrets and lies, resentments and anger, that form the foundation of our addiction. No one's comfortable with having to commit to paper our crimes, faults, false stories and untruths. This is the last chance to come clean and admit our wrongs, from insurance fraud to pocketing a lipstick from the beauty store.

Now is the time to let go of all the pretence and stories we tell ourselves and others about our lives. I'm beginning to see I never tell the truth - I always lie. Starting with granddad's secret. Covering my tracks and what he was doing. Not wanting to be found out and get into trouble. Knowing deep down what was happening to me was wrong and fretting I'd be held accountable and punished. Simultaneously I was hiding the shame that I didn't want it to stop because it made me feel special. I wanted the attention and what I thought was love so much.

I lied about my family. I told anyone who asked that I was happy and our family was happy. I hid that most of the time I felt frightened and alone. Not just because of my father's moods and his angry outbursts but also because of the way he treated my mother. I remember a week when my parents were happy, they were chatty, touching each other's arms, bumping shoulders at the kitchen bench. My mother was smiling, a lot and it terrified me. I had no idea how to respond or what it meant. I was finally able to relax when things went back to normal.

I acted as if I was unaffected by the bullying and name-calling at school. I kept a straight face when my hand was strapped because the teacher thought I was lazy for not passing the weekly spelling test. As an adult I learnt I was, in fact, dyslexic.

Lying, pretending, saying what I thought people wanted to hear, spinning a good story were all means of my survival. I didn't lie to trick or deceive, my motivation was purely self-protection, to stay safe, in world I didn't trust or feel comfortable inhabiting. It was a hazardous balancing act between being telling the truth or fabricating a plausible story. I became a master at creating the plausible story.

My wedding, arranged by my parents and the parents of my then-boyfriend was part of the fabric of lies that continued to grow around me. I was seventeen and pregnant, my boyfriend was nineteen. Not only were we too young to make a commitment to the baby and each other, it wasn't what we wanted. Our lives together were a sham and the only truth that ever came out of that relationship was when the divorce was granted.

I might have got my life together, I might have grown up and matured, done some self-reflection and personal growth. I might have made friends with people who gave me support and brought out the best in me or acted as role models and showed me how I could talk about my childhood abuse and heal. But they weren't the people I felt comfortable with or attracted into my life. I felt more a home with secrets and lies, bullies and those who reminded me of my father, his anger and control, and the dynamics I had observed in my parents' relationship.

My first violent partner had the character traits and personality I was familiar with. We were two frightened, angry, abused women looking for love and while we were attracted to each other and mirrored each other's childhoods, it didn't make for a loving, caring relationship. We were both damaged and desperately needy. She threw the first punch and controlled the relationship for the next five years.

A new secret, a new shame, more embarrassment and humiliation. I had cover stories to explain the bruises, broken bones and black eyes. Deep inside I felt responsible but didn't know how to escape. And while the biggest secret I kept was that my abuser was a woman, the greater lie is when society tells us we should leave a domestic violence situation and that life will be better. It wasn't better; it was hell.

I didn't know who I was, I didn't know how to live without fear, I'd lost the ability to make decisions, and was always second-guessing myself. I lived in fear, not trusting myself or anyone else. I jumped when someone knocked at the door. I was scared of the dark. I suffered from flashbacks and panic attacks. I tried to live as if everything had gone back to normal but it hadn't. I was numb and a shaking box of nerves. I couldn't sleep. I was frightened to leave the house. The outside world terrified me. I drank and took drugs, pretending I was managing. But I wasn't.

The need to hold everything at bay, to stop the pain and keep up the pretence meant I needed more and more alcohol, more and more drugs. I bought alcohol and drugs when I didn't have the money, skimping on groceries, running out of food. Stealing shoes and clothing for my sons. I lost my temper and attacked before I could get hurt, argued instead of talking things over. I lied about everything, childhood, relationships, the welfare of my two sons, if I was coping with my life.

This is what I've been tasked to put down on paper. Finding perspective and seeing the big picture. Finding the patterns of behaviour that keep me trapped in my addiction. Where I've been selfish and not taken responsibility for myself and my actions. The damage I've done to my children. I have to write it all down and find who I am now, who I've become and with this rigorous self-appraisal and honesty, I hope to find the beginning of self-acceptance and love.

16

The staff don't normally join us for morning or afternoon tea, they have their own staff room. So, when one of the therapists causally sits down beside me on the garden steps with a drink in one hand and a biscuit in the other, I'm both curious and a little nervous.

We sit in silence enjoying the break and the sun, watching a group playing hacky sack on the far side of the gardens. Of the four or five staff who attend Group, this woman is not one for idle chatter or being overly friendly. When she does speak, it's to the point and in a rather brisk manner. I can't image why she's here.

When she finally decides to speak I'm genuinely surprised by what she has to say. This afternoon Charles had been insisting we start taking daily Antabuse. Antabuse is a drug that makes you violently sick if you drink alcohol. He'd called it a precautionary measure for early recovery and stated that those who refused weren't taking their sobriety seriously. Much to his annoyance, I'd turned down his offer.

Now, this therapist is agreeing with my decision and saying I don't need the medication because she believes I'll remain sober for life. According to the statistics, maybe the only one in the whole group. My problem, she says, isn't alcohol or drugs, its relationship addiction. I'm stunned and try to process how everything I've done up until now has been founded on being an alcoholic and drug addict.

She goes on to explain that co-dependent addicts have little or no personal boundaries, they lack self-esteem, lose themselves in their relationships, and end up taking emotional and physical responsibility for their partner, to the detriment of their personal well-being because they fear the loss of the relationship.

I'm thinking, thinking, trying to come to terms with all she's saying. There's something familiar about her words, something lurking in the back of my mind and I'm scrambling to find it. She's right; I do this, I let go of who I am, my ideas, thoughts, values, even Self, trying to keep everything under control, nursing my partner's ego, not wanting to cause a problem, upset them, make them annoyed and possibly angry or violent. Coming out of these relationships not knowing who I am, having merged to the extent that their wishes and goals become my wishes and goals, and I don't know where they ended and I started.

I'm struggling for words, why hasn't this come up before? Why isn't this addressed in Group or one of the many counselling sessions? Surly this is important to many of us, not just to me?

The therapist can see my confusion and suggests I follow her. We walk back into the hospital, down the corridor, past the nurse's station and into the video room. Memories of weekend movie binging come to mind as I settle myself on the lumpy couch. There's a video already in the machine and after talking through the stack of videos and books in front of me on the coffee table, I'm left alone.

The videos contain a variety of relationship examples, pointing out the dysfunctional and co-dependence of each. There's lectures given by a professional standing on a stage and taking to a live audience, diagrams, coloured charts, facts and figures. There's scripted family and relationship scenes and before I hit overload, I switch off the machine and sit back down.

I grasp the overall concept but can see there's a lot more to it than the simplicity of giving up alcohol and drugs, unless I want to remain unattached for the rest of my life. But there's also an aspect of abstinence, taking time out and understanding where the pattern for my relationships come from.

The terminology is off-putting. I need to get my head around the new jargon, learn the meaning and behaviour of people-pleasing, being a caretaker, being unaware of my needs while being excessively dependent on others and having a heightened sense of fear around losing the relationship.

The first book I browse is on boundaries. I read a list of unhealthy boundaries and the list of healthy ones. I examine the lists closer and realise I don't have boundaries. I stumble over what happens if you have boundaries as opposed to not having boundaries. I try to think back, did anyone ever talk about them, at home or school? Boundaries sound similar to my brick wall. A sentence catches my attention, mentioning the lack of boundaries between a parent and child. Or maybe a grandfather and granddaughter?

I know I'm reading about myself. These types of relationships where I live my partner's life, obsess about them, try to anticipate all their needs and wants, turning myself inside out to please them, becoming a chameleon in my attempts to match their emotional state.

I'm ashamed to realise all my relationships have been unhealthy. As a child with my grandfather, trying to foresee my father's moods, knowing too much about my parents' relationship because of what mum shared with me. My adult relationships that always started out fun, romantic, with the chemical combustion of lust and over time felt unsafe and out of control. Most had a degree of being verbally and physically violent.

It's not that I didn't recognise something was wrong, I did. I just didn't know what. I'd start by trying to figure out what I was doing wrong and turn myself into a pretzel to make it right. Then I'd agonise over the relationship trying to fix it. Trying harder and harder and harder until my whole existence revolved around repairing the relationship and managing my partner. It never worked and I never felt safe or loved. It was always walking on a tightrope, knowing at any moment I could fall. At its worst I needed medical attention, and occasionally I'd feel like I was needed and loved which was preferable to being alone.

I shut the book and let it fall into my lap. It's all so much to take in. I close my eyes and rest my head back against the couch. I don't believe it was ever a conscious thought but when I was a child I felt if I brought in the washing or did the dishes or swept the floor or peeled the potatoes, at least my mother needed me even if she didn't love me.

17

It's not a secret anymore. But for a long time it was. I was deeply embarrassed and ashamed that my first lesbian relationship was manipulative, controlling and toxic. I concealed the truth for a long time because of my embarrassment at being terrorised and beaten by a woman.

Some of it was pride, of course, I was afraid I'd be judged. I was a feminist, active in the Woman's Movement, on the collective of the Women's Shelter, giving my time as a volunteer and helping women escape from violent husbands and bringing them into the safety of our local halfway house. It took me years to admit I was one of them, a *battered wife*.

At the time my understanding of the Women's Movement political thought on female to female domestic violence was it shouldn't be discussed or put on the agenda because it was opposed to the political line being pushed by the majority of white, middle-class feminists that men were the rapists, wife beaters, perpetrators of family violence. Men were being portrayed as the patriarchy's brutal foot soldiers. Women were being depicted as nurturers, mothers, givers of life, linked to the ancient Mother

Goddess religions demonstrating the virtues of beauty, love, sexuality, motherhood, creativity, fertility and healing. Lesbian domestic abuse and female violence was to be addressed later, when women won equality.

Much closer to home was the assumption when I turned up to see the doctor that I'd been beaten by my husband. I remember getting into a taxi home after a hospital visit, and being told by the kindly male taxi driver that I 'should leave the bastard'. When I did make an appointment to see a counsellor about a controlling partner, she also assumed I was there about an abusive husband.

Encouraged by friends to escape, I did leave my partner several times. However, being harassed by phone, being yelled at from the street and suffering several broken windows soon saw the invitation to seek refuge with friends being retracted.

I stopped being an activist. I stopped attending collective meetings. I stopped seeing the majority of my friends. I sold my car. Life became completely focused on her moods, her needs, her friends. It was simpler to be friends with other women who maintained abusive relationships. Everybody understood and there were no questions asked.

Now we come to the confession, the twist in the story. I didn't ultimately leave, taking my children and what we could carry, jumping into a friend's van, making our escape while she was at work because I thought she was going to finally kill me, although there were plenty of times when I thought that might happen.

I left because I thought I might *kill her*.

18

Under the oppressive weight of the queen-size mattress, in claustrophobic darkness, barely able to breath, I revert to type and surrender. I'm not supposed to. That's not the object of this psychodrama performance. I'm supposed to fight for my sobriety and portray the struggle over my addiction by throwing off the mattress and the people sitting around the edge, to reclaim my life.

It's been suggested we use our voice as well as our arms, legs and body to free ourselves. But I lie still, feeling no urgency to raise my voice, try to fight, make a fuss or in any other way throw off the weight of the innerspring or anyone sitting on it.

The group have been told their mother is under the mattress and this is their chance for revenge, so don't let her escape. I feel no animosity toward these mother-haters, I understand all too well. I hated my mother for years and I'm sure my sons hate me.

I'm on my back, arms and legs pinned, head turned to the side, not feeling afraid or in danger. It's peaceful and comforting, lying trapped in darkness. My whole life I've felt like this, immobilised, stuck, powerless and restrained by conditioning and circumstance.

A head appears, telling me to breath, to fight, to yell and scream, to kick myself free. It's Ted, with his wispy beard, oversized shirt and striped trousers making him look more like a hippy than a licensed psychodramatist and professional director.

I think about what he's said but don't move. On one level I can't be bothered, on another I don't have anything to prove and I know the hospital won't let me die. I just don't feel like doing as expected, in yet another situation where I'm resistant to authority.

Suddenly, I'm screaming at the top of my lungs and fighting against the mattress with all my might, trying to push up with my hands and feet. I don't have the strength and I can't get any traction. I collapse and try to twist and turn onto my side, thinking if I can get up on my hands and knees I could push up with my back.

I'm enraged. I can feel my heart racing, my face and neck surging with heat and I have to take deep breaths. I'm seeing *him* and *his* beckoning finger, feeling the waves of shame and fear as *he* reaches into my knickers and I look over my shoulder to where daddy left the room to talk to my grandmother, shutting the door behind him.

The image in my mind changes and I feel sick, my stomach churning, as I defend myself against *her*. I can feel *her* fists pummelling my breasts, hands slapping, nails raking my face. I yell and call out, wrestling the ghosts and shadows of the past. My head is pounding with fury and resentment, I feel as if it's about to explode. I can't bear this any longer, this constant overwhelming feeling of weakness and vulnerability.

I fight harder, not letting anything stop me. I begin to feel freedom and see light and push toward it, taking deeper breaths as I emerge into the blinding brilliance of the sunny room.

I roll over and lie panting, sweat dribbling into my eyes and stinging. I rest my hands on my chest, exhausted. When I open my eyes I'm surrounded with grinning, smiling, laughing faces. I can't understand what they're saying but I know they're talking, their mouths opening and closing. Ted is kneeling beside me, putting his arm around my shoulders, helping me to sit up. When I catch my breath I stand on wobbly legs and limp back to my chair.

I'm reading back over what I've just written and wondering, have I captured it all, what happened, how it felt, what I was thinking, the intense experience under the mattress. It seemed profound or maybe that's too big a word. Maybe, it's like the anger exercise, I've been able to let go more resentment, more hopelessness. Perhaps now I'll be able to forgive myself.

I take a moment to look up from my journal and notice how many people are walking in the grounds, sitting under trees and playing ball games on the lawn. That's not the way I refresh my energy. I need quiet and refection to recharge. People's energy wears me out.

I turn the page and think about what else happened at the afternoon psychodrama session. I can almost still feel his presence beside me. He'd sat on one corner of the mattress determined his mother would learn what it felt like to be held captive with no way out and no one coming to save her.

When I returned to my seat Ted asked for feedback on my drama. A couple of the young women hadn't moved from their chairs and said they found it frightening to watch. They thought Ted should have stopped the drama, especially when it seemed I wasn't moving and to them it seemed like a long time. Someone talked about the fear they had experienced as the men had moved closer together, holding down the edge when the mattress started to move. She said she'd wanted to run and help me.

A couple of the men thought it was funny, a bit of a game, until they thought about some of the things that happened to them in childhood.

Soul Connection

Moving into foster homes and putting up with kids from other families, when their mother shacked up with a step-father who didn't like them. Women of all kinds were lumped together as being bad mothers.

An older man was the last to speak. He said he was sorry. His eyes were tearing up and threatening to spill. Memories filled his mind of being a little boy, shut in his bedroom for wetting his bed, left at a stranger's house and abused when his mother went out. He remembered being left in a hospital room, needing a plaster cast for a broken arm and just wanting his mother to come in and hold his hand. As the memories came back and took over, every time he saw the mattress move he jumped on it. He was so angry, so enraged about his mother's treatment of him I just wanted to kill her myself and never let her out from under the mattress.

Ted calls us up to the front of the group and asks the man to hug his mother, asking me to hug my son. We start with a tentative hold, bodies rigid, arms stiff. Ted talks about the ideal relationship between a mother and her son. He gets us to conjure up how we'd wanted our real mothers to love and respond to us. How would it feel? He talks about sons and what they want from those mothers, how would it feel?

As we hug again, I close my eyes and cling to my sons. Feeling their muscular bodies, smelling their manliness, their size and height towering over me. I can feel my sons hugging me, holding me tight and I respond to their warmth. I hear Ted's voice saying more and more, hold tighter, hug deeper, more, more. As I drink in my beloved sons, I never want to let them go. Tears fill my eyes and fall down my face, and all my anguish over them leaving, walking away pours out of me.

We break apart, still touching shoulders, crying. As I walk back to my seat the man picks up his chair and pushes it in beside me, taking my hand. It feels warm, rough and thick, a man's hand, his grip tight and comforting. I feel I could walk through fire with him holding my hand.

19

I don't know which is worse, the outrage or the uncontrollable tears. I feel so angry, so indignant, I'm about to explode. At the same time I feel small, used and traumatised. I'm trying to write what happened and how it has left me feeling but I don't seem able to get the words out. I don't know what to say or where to start. I just know it wasn't okay, it shouldn't have happened. It was wrong.

I'm woken in the middle of the night with someone shaking my shoulder. I'm told to hurry and get dressed. I pull on my clothes by the small wedge of light coming in from the corridor. There's no time to ask questions as the nurse rushes ahead of me. Around the corner of the corridor she slows and putting her shoulder to the door, enters.

The room is in semi-darkness, the only occupied bed is surrounded by a huddle of uniformed staff. Whatever is happening is obviously serious. There's a small portable tank by the bed with a face mask dangling over the cart handle which I guess is oxygen. The atmosphere is tense and when the nurse points to a chair I'm happy to drag it away from the bed and sit down.

Soul Connection

This is clearly an unused ward. The white, steel-framed beds with rolled and tied plastic-covered mattresses have been pushed to one side, the small chest of drawers stacked against the wall and the blinds have been pulled down. The only light is the shaded bulb above the patient's headboard.

I honestly don't know why I'm here or what I'm supposed to do. I have no nursing experience or knowledge of first aid. I'm not sure if I know the patient and if that might be the reason I'm here. Other than that, I'm at a loss to understand my presence in the room.

There's a hushed conversation, a decision reached and the team exit, taking the oxygen tank with them. The nurse gives me a quick rundown on what's happening. The woman is an ex-patient and she's been drinking all weekend, causing alcohol poisoning and life-threatening seizures. Her husband has left her, effectively ending their fifteen-year marriage. I'm to alert the emergency team if she has another seizure. The nurse hands me the alarm bell, a black rubber-covered buzzer attached to the bed head by an electrical cord. With a nod of her head she leaves, closing the door behind her.

I sit as if turned to stone with the closing of the door, trying to understand what just happen. I'm alone in a disused ward responsible for the life of a seriously ill patient. My only instruction to press the buzzer and summon an emergency team. It's the middle of the night, the rest of the hospital is sleeping and I'm sitting watch.

I feel my eyes have gone dry I'm watching the mound of white embossed cotton cover so intently. I have to force my eyes to blink, so frightened am I that I might miss a movement in the bed and the woman will die. The rubber buzzer in my hand is slippery with sweat while my legs and feet are so cold I have cramp.

At first I don't realise the silence has been broken and then it finally dawns on me the bed is moving, shaking. The white covered patient is jerking, jumping and the bed seems to be moving. I frantically press the alarm, waiting for the emergency scream of bells from the corridor but there's only silence. I press again and again but still nothing. Afraid the bell is broken, I rush out into the corridor and yell. Thankfully I hear the sound of pounding feet coming closer. It's not until I gasp I realise I've been holding my breath.

The emergency team burst through the door and immediately go into action. I creep slowly away until I bump into one of the beds and half fall, half sit, watching in sheer terror. Within minutes they're gone again. Their parting words are to press the bell once a light flashes in the nurse's station.

As the door closes I can feel the rising panic. I begin to pace up and down. I can't believe I'm being left here to go through this again. With clenched fists I turn at the far wall and try to slow both my breathing and my footsteps. Even in the middle of the night there must be someone, anyone, with medical experience who could be in this poor woman's room. Someone who'd be more help than me.

I go to the window and sneak a peek behind the blind. There's the first signs of dawn. A shiver runs down my spine. All these years later and the chill of a new day still drags me back to the horror of that maternity hospital run by those narrow-minded old hags. I was eighteen and having my first baby. Gossip had spread the details of my pregnancy, the shotgun wedding and my mother's refusal to help or support me because of the disgrace and embarrassment to the family.

I was shunted into a side ward and left on my own with only the most senior of staff attending me. For forty-eight hours I lay alone, unsure of what was happening, frightened and only checked on for routine observation of the baby's heartbeat and toilet visits. The father-to-be was sent away and told he'd be rung when there was news.

When I did ring the bell to go to the toilet it was to walk behind a screen pushed along by a nurse. I felt isolated, intimidated by the screen-holding and panicked by my ignorance of the labour and birthing process. When my mother had given birth she'd disappear while we were sleeping and dad had told us of the baby's arrival over breakfast. This was very different.

My eldest child, my firstborn son, arrived after a difficult delivery a minutes after midnight and weighted exactly 10 pounds. My doctor hadn't been called because the matron didn't think it was fair to disturb the poor man at such an ungodly hour. While she later acknowledged it might have been better if I'd had a caesarean, in the end, she said with a shrug, things had turned out alright. When my doctor made his rounds the next morning the only reference to the birth was to say, at his size, my son would make a good All Blacks rugby player one day.

Sitting now, huddled with a blanket around me, I can still remember the staggering indifference of the women in that country hospital. The shame and disgrace I felt. The ever-present injustice of their judgement, the snide remarks. The total indifference toward an inexperienced young mother having her first child and the lasting impression they left on my life.

My body feels heavy slumped in the chair, my mind drifting over the events of several decades. I'm amazed as always by the physicality of memories, how they not only remain in the mind but how their echo remains in the body.

When there's movement in the bed, I'm on my feet, pressing the alarm bell and then letting it drop to the floor. I rush to the bed and pull back the blankets, pushing the woman onto her side, as the emergency team charge through the door. They elbow me out of the way and go to work, one kneeling on the bed, another sorting out the oxygen tank. And then, without a word, they're gone again.

I resume my seat, rewrapping my legs, pushing my hands under the blanket over my knees and into their warmth. I can hear the woman's even breathing and I wonder what it takes to break sobriety, in her case the end of a long marriage. What would need to happen for me to pick up a drink, to break my resolve, I wonder. The death of a son, a grandchild? A diagnosis of cancer or some other life-threatening illness, would that turn me back into a drunk?

I'm startled when a head pops around the door and tells me to go and get breakfast.

THE WEEKEND

I am not responsible for my disease
but I am responsible for my behaviour.

20

The hospital is in lockdown. Windows are closed and must remain that way. Doors have towels wrapped around the latches to prevent slamming. There's to be no running in the corridors. Outside, the rose garden is off-limits. There's no ball games, singing or musical instruments. All group activities are postponed and outdoor conversation is to be kept at a whisper.

This is a prevention measure for the patient suffering from alcohol poisoning and having seizures. She isn't improving and the seizures can be triggered by sudden loud noise. The usual busy weekend hospital has become silent and lifeless.

I haven't told anyone about my vigil in the night. I haven't talked about the distress of being left in that room alone with a woman having fits and needing medical intervention. I'm not sure why. It's like so many of the traumatic events I've experienced, it's been consigned to a box and put on the shelf.

Like so many boxes on that shelf, I treated it as normal. The sexual abuse, the violent relationships, the angry father and dysfunctional family. It's just normal. Being attracted to toxic, controlling people with a disposition for control and taking their temper out on others. Normal.

I thought one of the staff might have taken me aside and checked how I was feeling. But nobody did. I could have brought it up in Group or one of the counselling sessions. But I didn't. I could have taken Father William aside and talked to him. I could have demanded to know why I was chosen to be hauled out of bed in the middle of the night and left in charge of a patient whose life hung in the balance. But I didn't.

I absorbed it into my life as one more incident in a life full of traumatic happenings. Am I ready to acknowledge the trauma and face the contents of the boxes I've stacked and called my life? Will sobriety be the opportunity to empty the boxes and clear the shelves? Perhaps then I won't need it anymore.

WEEK FOUR

Most alcoholics would rather die than learn anything about themselves. In fact, they do.

21

It's just after seven and I'm dressing in a borrowed pair of men's striped pyjamas and holding a nursery rhyme style Wee Willy Winky candle holder made from cardboard and a saucer from the dining room. The only reason I'm doing this cold stone sober is because this evening's fancy dress party is compulsory.

It's customary in the final week of the program for the staff to host a costume party. It's a taste of a sober social gathering. Dressing up, having to dance and make small talk is meant to push us outside our comfort zones. We're attending an event without the lubricant of alcohol or drugs.

The main hall is decorated with colourful streamers, balloons and a mirrored disco ball. There's music, a drinks table, and generous supper tables set out around the walls. Most of the costumes are simple, quickly thrown together affairs that we only had the afternoon to prepare. I see lots of sexy prostitutes, angels with wings and glitter make up, an assortment of super heroes, cowboys, pirates, nurses, doctors with stereoscopes around their necks, clergy, pointy-horned devils and a collection of Grim Reapers with a range of black cardboard scythes. Father William has offered his theory about our subconscious making our decision to dress as good or evil.

At the drinks table we're downing fruit punch like it'll give us that congeniality we're used to when drinking our usual tipple. Naturally it's not having the effect we're used to when we're in a crowd with loud music. However, standing at the bar and drinking is still a habit we haven't broken.

I wasn't a regular pub drinker. I might call in with friends on the way to a club but I normally drank at home. I wasn't a social drinker, needing people around to give me either a reason or an excuse to drink, I was happy to drink alone. I didn't enjoy the taste of alcohol, I wasn't a wine connoisseur. I drank purely to erase the emotional pain, the self-hatred and inferiority issues I had. I drank to block out the reality I found myself in during the violent relationships and afterwards to handle who I'd become because of those relationships.

My grandfather was an alcoholic. Part of my father's family story is granddad and his four brothers pissing away their inheritance. They went to war twice and returned traumatised and drinking hard. Granddad told stories of the wine and women in France. In his seventies, because of diabetes, he had first a foot and then the leg amputated. It didn't interfere with his drinking.

My mother told stories of my father's drinking in their early marriage. She told us he was a belligerent, angry drunk who started fights, a brawler who wouldn't let an argument go. At some point she'd been able to get him to stop and I never knew him to have more than a couple of beers in summer. That's not to say there wasn't alcohol in the house; there was a high cupboard in the kitchen stocked with hard liquor, never wine. All of my childhood I knew dad to be a gambler, betting on the horses and the weekly raffles drawn on national television.

Dad loved the trots and it was a special outing to be taken to a twilight meeting. I loved seeing the horses, the excitement, the jockey colours, the buzz of the crowd. Dad knew some of the trainers and as a special treat he'd take me around back to the stables where I could pat the big furry heads hanging over the stable doors.

There's been some discussion in Group about alcoholism and drug addiction as a genetic or family issue. So many of us have parents and grandparents with addiction problems. In one of the counselling sessions we'd drawn our addiction family tree. On my paternal side I was able to identify my grandfather and his brothers as alcoholics and my father as an alcoholic and gambler. After reading more about co-dependence I put my mother down as an enabler. As the oldest child I'm an alcoholic, drug addict and enabler.

From what little I know about my brothers and sisters I was able to record gamblers, exercise addicts, enablers, alcoholics, and workaholics. I know my sons have their own issues around alcohol and drugs. I understand myself to be the child of an alcoholic who is also the child of an alcoholic. I fear for my sons and my grandchildren.

Charles has told us we are breaking the family pattern. I hope so. It would be wonderful to think I could be the generation to stop the disease described in one of the books I'm reading as '*the family disease*', because of the way it's passed on through learned behaviour and genetics. It's helping me realise I didn't become an addict in a vacuum. I have our family disease and genetics.

Looking at the large sheet of butcher's paper spread out on the floor with the names of my family spreading like tree branches, I begin to see other patterns. My mother always wanting to lose ten pounds, my yo-yo dieting since I started full time work at sixteen, my sisters being long term Weight Watch members. The fitness fanatics, the workaholics, the gamblers, the shopaholics, the enablers and co-dependent wives. The

Soul Connection

abusive relationships. And those who married into families with the same dysfunctions, displaying the same pattens.

If I take my butcher's paper and put it alongside each of my sibling's addiction trees and each of their spouse's addiction trees and so on... I could cover the floor of this room and the floor of the hospital and the country...

Someone is elbowing me in the side, and I look up into the eyes of a stranger. I give a tentative smile with no knowledge as to who the woman is. She tells me about her week in hospital and the near death experience she had. I stare into her face remembering that cold and lonely night in the unused ward room. She's dressed as a Goth, a black wig, black clothes and black lipstick. Her eyes are ringed in Kohl pencil, her nails in black vanish, and she's wearing men's work boots.

I try to match this image in my mind to that of a distorted, distressed, middle-aged woman whose husband walked out the door after many years of marriage. I thought there might have been children, a pet, a dog. I imagined upset neighbours reflecting on the once-happy couple. She yells "Thank you!" at me as she hurries back to the dance floor.

I marvel at her ability to bounce back when I've yet to get started. I'm counting down the days until I leave all this and have to go it alone. I was so afraid of coming into the hospital and participating in the program and now I'm just as afraid to leave.

22

I stumble out of Father William's house in a state of emotional exhaustion, across the lawn and fall to my hands and knees. When I look up it's into the beatific smile of a blue-robed plaster Virgin Mary, arms extended in supplication.

I'm nauseous and dizzy, my legs feel jelly-like and I fall a second time when I try to stand. The world is spinning and I let my head drop in an effort to regain my equilibrium. After several steadying deep breaths, I find I can stand. I don't know what I expected at completion of my Fifth Step but this reaction has taken me completely by surprise.

Choosing the person to hear your Fifth Step is very important, that's been stressed in Group. A Catholic priest wouldn't have been my first thought as I read the list of locals willing to take on the role of confessor. There were teachers and professionals, a retired dental clinician, numerous A.A. members, churchgoers from a variety of denominations and those that considered themselves as neutral. My first choice would have been a Pagan lesbian but not seeing anyone like that listed, my thoughts turned to my teacher and sobriety. I'm in the program for alcohol and drug addiction, not as a lesbian looking to score political points. I want to restore my life with a spiritual foundation, making Father William the perfect choice. He is the humblest, most spiritual human being I've ever encountered.

His calmness, serenity and acceptance is something I want to attain. He seems so peaceful, without the need to predict and control. Sitting close to him in Group I can feel his tranquil energy. I know his spiritual beliefs are strong and I identify with his process of *'Handing Over'*; putting your fears, doubts and needs into the hands of something bigger than ourselves.

I'm able to visualise those cupped hands and imagine heaping all my anxiety and self-doubt into them. Knowing they're ready to receive everything I can't manage. Turning my will over, the care of my children, my recovery and having a connection with the energy that's all around us.

I wait and allow my eyes to adjust to the fading light. The mountains look so far away, the sky a pale pink in the setting sun. The valley is already in shadow, the villages hidden but for the glow of street lamps and the blue flicker of televisions.

It's an ordinary evening, on an ordinary day. People came home from work, children arrived back from school. And an addict has unburdened herself by telling one other person and her spiritual-self, *the exact nature of her wrongs.*

I've admitted the wrongs against family, children, friends, the community, neighbours and passers-by. I've made a clean and honest acknowledgement of my transgressions and exposed my gifts and my frailties. I'm ready to truly begin my recovery with a clear conscience.

I don't know how I'm supposed to feel. Do I feel differently, having declared the actions and behaviours that led to the guilt and shame I've carried for so long? Will I feel lighter and more able to look people in the face? Will I smile and feel happier meeting new people and making new friends? Will people see me differently? Not that withdrawn, defensive, closed-off woman but perhaps a new version of myself? A woman with a bright aura, open hearted, walking forward instead of sidestepping away.

I stare intently into the Virgin Mary's face. She's caught in concrete, immoveable, stuck like I was. Caught in the same old thoughts, the same old thinking and behaviour. All the patterns that held me prisoner. If She could speak would it be with compassion? Would She recognise my repentance and remorse? Would She grant me the forgiveness Father William did with his final words;

"Welcome back to humanity, Hannah."

23

The world I inhabit when I'm asleep is as real to me as the world outside these four walls. Within the safe warmth of my bed I experience my life in a different realm. I see it in my first language, in pictures and images. I connect with my deepest Self and change my daily life into symbols, archetypes and metaphors. Over the years I've kept dream diaries and recorded this language to learn and reflect on. Most of my dreams stay with me for the day, giving me time to replay them over and over again, gathering their meaning and immersing myself in the dream feeling and accompanying emotion.

Recovery has provided me with another recurring dream. In it I'm at a party and when I'm offered a drink or a joint I take it and within one sip or one toke I panic, throwing the glass or the joint to the floor. I begin shouting and explaining I'm sober, counting the days and now I have to start all over again because of the slip. My subconscious seems to be acting as my watchdog, reminding me over and over again of the promise I've made to myself, my sincere wish to be sober and change the habits of years.

Soul Connection

This is just one of the recurring dreams I have. The longest repetitive dream began when I was a child. In the darkness is a phone box with its light on. Outside in the impenetrable darkness is danger. Unknown and without a name, I know it's lurking there and I'm frightened. More than frightened, terrified. Fearful for my life and only someone's help will save me. I have to use the phone or I won't survive.

I have the receiver in my hand and when I open the fingers of my other hand the pennies I need for the call have disappeared. In a panic I feel in my pockets, I crouch down and look amongst the rubbish on the floor, chip packets, cigarette butts, dead matches and screwed up pieces of paper. I'm left whimpering in my sleep and wake in a state of alarm and near hysteria, heart racing and breathing erratic.

Over the years the phone box has disappeared and been replaced by a rotary dial desk phone. In this scenario, the tension of life and death is the same, but the dial won't turn, won't budge. Or I've forgotten the number I have to call, or I can't find the phone book to look up the number. Sometimes, I can't remember who it is I'm supposed to call, what their name is and I can't use the phone book. In the most frightening dreams the phone completely melts in my hand, the coloured wax dripping through my fingers.

While the dream plot has remained the same for over thirty years, my subconscious has kept up with the evolutional changes of the telecommunication devices. The dream I've woken from this morning had a dial tone on my mobile but I couldn't find the keypad. One moment it was there in plain sight and the next it was gone, leaving me stabbing at empty button holes. I recognise this dream as my anxiety dream. An alert to heightened apprehension and uncertainty. I'm fearful of leaving the warm compassion of the hospital and going back into the cold ambivalence of the outside world.

Four weeks ago I feared leaving home for the uncertainty of the hospital, staff, patients and the program. Now, I'm unsure about leaving the safety of the hospital and going back to the ambiguity of the new life I've chosen for myself. Again, it's not a question of will I stay alcohol and drug free - that's a given. However, will I be able to manage everything else that's required to start a new life without the props and crutches of my old life?

I need to turn away from those people who were once my 'using friends' and find a new support network with those in recovery and sobriety. I need to change habits and routines and develop new ways to cope with my anxiety and stress, nightmares and memories. Handing over, reflective journaling, giving up the illusion of control, reaching out to my children, old friends and immediate family is my priority now. I'm apprehensive about leaving and beginning this new journey.

I reach for my journal and record the dream, my apprehension and anxiety about the coming days. I jot down how the dream left me feeling and a brief reflection on that feeling. I also want to write a list of what I have to do when I'm finally back home. Ideas of how to deal with cravings, panic attacks, feeling headachy or nauseous. I've been thinking over who in my A.A. meeting I might approach about being my sponsor, so I scribble down some names. I have questions but have already developed a way to find answers.

I form my questions in such a way as to pose the very heart of the issue, with no doubt, uncertainty or ambiguity. I toss it to the universe and await the answer. The reply can come in a multitude of ways, in a dream, a word or passage in a book, a conversation in a film, video or television program. It may be a random conversation, a passage in a letter, a gift. The secret is to remain open and not be fooled by the wrapping or packaging in which the answer comes to you. Be careful what you ask for; 'I want a new home' might see your old one burn to the ground. In this regard I find my heightened observational skills, honed from being dyslexic, very beneficial when wanting to solve a problem.

Home in its many forms is another major trope that regularly turns up as a recurring dream. Finding a home, living in the structure of a home like a building site, not being able to leave home, being trapped by childhood, never having had an adult relationship and wanting one. In my dreams I have endless conversations with my parents about when will I be able to move on, to be married, to leave my childhood behind.

I'm taking note of this dream as I work on the childhood sexual abuse in counselling and in Group. There's times when I think of these dreams in terms of a social experiment of my subconscious awareness to learn what I'm not and what I am processing, healing and letting go. Water is representative of my emotions. Being in a boat or other unsinkable vessel bobbing about on moving water, the sea, a river. I think of these dreams as emotions I'm avoiding, not taking notice of or failing to heal from. Tidal waves or a calm lake tell their own story of my emotional state. I sketch the water and write a feeling under it, sometimes adding a colour. When I flick back over a week, a month, I get an impression of my emotions over time.

My lost sons are often in my dreams. I have conversations with them as I celebrate or mourn past events. I'm often trying to explain or alleviate my guilt at abandoning them. In my dreams they are seven and ten although in my conscious mind I know they are now young men. These dreams left me with a feeling of dread or longing that can last several days. At times the after-feeling is more telling that the images and action of the dream itself.

Having committed my dream and the fears it brought up into my journal and having scribbled my thoughts and To-Do lists without concern for grammar or spelling, my mind is clearer and my anxiety reduced. I close my journal, feeling ready for the day ahead, in a much better space to cope. I visualise the cupped hands and place in them all my worries and concerns for what is ahead. After telling myself *what happens is meant to happen*, I head to the shower.

24

I think of myself as a competent off-the-cuff speaker but really I'm not. I start strong but then tend to lose my way and waffle. So, I'm making notes for today's 'Passing Out' speech. Passing Out is the tongue-in-cheek name for our graduation.

Our graduation speech is compulsory and meant as a thank you to the staff and the others in our group. We're also expected to treat it like sharing in an A.A. Meeting and reflect on our time in the hospital and the program. I'm treating it like a before and after testimony.

Our graduation will be held in the hospital chapel with everyone invited, from the hospital Director to the kitchen staff. It's been mentioned by Charles that while we don't have to thank everyone by name, it is an expectation the staff that were part of our regular Group, counsellors and therapists, will expect to be called by their first names.

Formal group photographs will be taken by a professional and staff will make themselves available to those who make a request. We've already planned lots of personal snaps by those who thought to bring a camera, on the garden steps. There's been a flurry of final makeup and hair setting. There's a few suits and ties among the older men.

The hospital is putting on a special afternoon tea, cream sponges, iced cupcakes and none of the usual plates of plain biscuits. There's a ripple of excitement about the possibility of hot savouries.

The bus taking me home leaves at five o'clock. I've packed my bag and checked the wardrobe twice. I've swept the floor and wiped out the three drawers. I'm wearing my best gear, second pair of sandals and clutching my notes, sitting on the bed. The view from the window has become so familiar, the mown lawn, the few tall trees and a patch of sky.

I'm having difficulty remembering how I felt when I arrived thirty days ago. So much has happened. The cliche emotional rollercoaster ride. No amount of talking with ex-patients prepared me for such a personal journey. I came in oblivious to my disease and leave with a greater knowledge and more respect for the harm alcoholic and drug addiction causes, both to the addict and their family.

I had no understanding of coercive and co-dependent relationships when I arrived. And while I still have a lot of work to do, I at least know what I'm dealing with and my part in the dynamics of abusive and controlling partners.

One of my biggest take-aways is the reality of black-outs. I had periods of time when I couldn't remember where I'd been, who I'd seen or what I'd done. I'd be driving, the boys in the back seat, and not know if we were going shopping or coming home. Often, I didn't know if I was dropping the boys at school or had just picked them up. It frightened me to think how close I came to a car accident, with the possibility of injuring or killing my children. We'd been shown pictures of Black Out wards where addicts had to be told every morning where they were and who they were. After the night watching for alcoholic poisoning seizures and having little liver damage, I feel I've escaped the worst of the harm alcoholism can cause.

I have notes on my revived spiritual practice, the reconnection with my Inner Voice, the evening prayer for my sons' safety and the Twelve Steps. Plus, in the back of my mind Father William as inspiration and role model.

The hospital chapel is a thing of beauty. It's a circular domed building with the curved front windows in spectacular stained glass. On entering you can't help but be amazed at the warm light flooding in through the ruby, amber and jade glass. The polished rosewood pews, the red and gold carpet and above the pulpit, fluttering Alcoholics Anonymous saffron fringed banners.

There's a general buzz of excitement as the final preparations are completed and the microphone adjusted. We are awed as we slide into our seats, peering around, pointing to friends from other groups, staff we know and giggling at the photographer wrestling with a number of long lens cameras and lighting stands.

When the Director walks to the front holding his speech notes, takes his glasses from his jacket pocket and slips them on, the room becomes quiet. Gossip has already informed us the Director is a recovering alcohol and heroin user but this is the first time I've heard him share his story. It's obvious why he holds the position he does; he's the perfect fit. He talks about the staff and their dedication to giving back, his commitment, motivation and personal vision for the hospital.

The sharing is heartfelt and emotional. There's tears, applauding and hugs all round. I feel grateful and encouraged when I stand and ready myself to walk down the aisle, running my fingers through my hair, adjusting my shirt.

"Hi, I'm Hannah and I'm an alcoholic and drug addict."

25

I hit my personal rock bottom the day the kitten died. Hitting rock bottom is characterised as being where things can't get any worse or being at your lowest possible point. And while it is a generalised term for having to face your addiction, perhaps being arrested, hurting someone while high or having an overdose scare, it wasn't the day I stopped using alcohol and drugs. That was still some years away, however, it was the day I stopped pretending I was doing anything other than merely surviving.

Holding the still warm, lifeless body in my arms, the world stopped. I was standing on the side of the road, in front of the old, battered van I lived in, and the farmer who had slowed his tractor to ask if I needed help had moved off.

My mind went blank. I was confused about what had just happened, unable to register the offer of help with the death of the kitten. She'd been my companion for the last few months, a time-wasting endless ball of fluffy fun. She sat beside me at meals, trying to hook food off my plate with her paw. She crawled into my bed, body curled tight to my own, her purring soothing us both. And now she was gone.

I don't know how long I stood there, the body cooling, my mind not functioning, my stomach reeling, my legs turned to stone. I tried to work out what to do next. In my head I saw flickering images of caves and holes dug in the ground, heaped stone cairns, white crosses and grave stones, cemeteries with black clothed mourners. None of the pictures made sense. I had no idea how to dispose of the body of the last living thing I was attached to. If I put the kitten down, in the ground and covered her up, I would be utterly and completely alone.

No home, no letter box for the mail, no telephone to talk on, no rooms, no doors to walk in and out of. No children. Everything gone. Just the decrepit old van with its leaky roof and stuffed gearbox. The single mattress and second-hand blankets, the plastic bag of clothes, the blue rain coat and sand shoes, the bits of old crockery and coloured picnic cutlery set.

When I tried to see into the future there was only darkness. There was no tomorrow, not even a tonight. There was nothing, no forward, no backwards, no moving beyond this moment. It wasn't that I wanted to harm myself or end my life. I wasn't having suicidal thoughts. I didn't want to kill myself. I just didn't know how to live now the kitten was dead. Not that I'd been exactly living.

I was homeless, living in an old camping van, driving aimlessly around the country, staying away from the main roads, sometimes staying at camping grounds, sometimes parking beside a river, or simply parking on the side of the road. I had a gas ring and kettle, a fortnightly government payment and bought alcohol and drugs, petrol, kitten mince and occasionally, when I could afford it, food.

I wasn't in contact with anyone. I didn't know where my sons were living and didn't let myself think about it. I wasn't unhappy or sad or worried or fearful or anxious; all those things would have needed conscious thought while I preferred to drifted through the days in a wasted and intoxicated state. I didn't have a plan, believed I wasn't hurting anyone and as long as one day continued to follow the next, I didn't anticipate stopping. Until the kitten died.

Out of this dark place came a thought. Faced with a decision between life and death, I always chose death. Not in its most literal term, I don't want to end my life or kill myself. But when faced with a choice between positive and negative, I always chose the negative. A rough path or smooth path, I chose the rough. If I knew something would be good for me, I turned my back. If someone offered help, support or friendship, I refused and walked away. It was as if I needed to repeatedly punish myself, prove my unworthiness, my shame and guilt. To validate I was undeserving and unlovable. To prove I had no value and nothing to offer the world.

In that moment I decided I was going to choose life, not death. I was going to live, not merely survive. I was going to make changes that led to health not destruction. I saw myself as if through the end of a telescope, a lonely, displaced woman continuing to self-harm years after the childhood suffering had ended. From now on I'd value myself. I'd make choices that reflected self-love not self-loathing. I'd stop self-sabotaging and start believing in myself.

Here I am today, standing before you a graduate of this program, in recovery, making a life-long commitment to myself and my sobriety.

THE WEEKEND

What other people think of me is none of my business.

26

When I arrived home from the hospital I sat down and didn't think I'd ever stand up again. I was mentally and emotionally exhausted. My brain hurt, my mind was shattered and every muscle in my body ached. I stared out the window at nothing, surrounded by all my belongings, a nest of emotional comfort. My time in the hospital rolled around in my head on a loop, events, sessions, Group, flashing on and off. I was unable to think or move, my mind and body weighted down by all that had taken place over the last thirty days.

I slept in my own bed at last, comforted by my desk in the corner and the looming old wardrobe. I cooked in my own kitchen and ate out on the veranda watching the horses, noticing the changes in the garden and the fruit trees. I came in when the sun sank behind the mountains and got up when the sun rose. I played with the stack of books I wanted to read, opening them on my lap and forgetting about them, before opening them again. I doodled in my journal, funny line drawings that made no sense. I was listless and made no plans.

Soul Connection

Weeks later, I started weekly counselling sessions for the sexual abuse and returned to my local A.A. meetings. It was like my brain was addled and after a few hours concentration I needed to rest. My dreams were frightening; I'd be at a party and drink a glass of wine, waking in terror that I'd started drinking again. I'd run out of the supermarket in a panic leaving my half-filled trolley behind. If I left the house for more than two hours I imagined the house would be gone when I got home.

One day I picked up my journal and began to write. I filled page after page, the scribbling getting faster and faster, less and less readable, until, exhausted, I dropped my pen and burst into tears. I cried until my eyes ran dry and my head was throbbing. I threw the journal off the veranda, over the fence into the horse paddock and snapped my pen in two. I couldn't contain my rage and began to scream, imagining myself once more trapped under the queen sized mattress and needing air.

When I calmed down I made myself a hot drink and went back to the comfortable chair on the veranda. I felt unnerved, out of control. I wasn't sure how I felt, what I thought. I didn't know who I was or who I wanted to become. My life felt like a mess and I desperately wanted it to go back to normal.

I remembered Father William's spiritual class and lay down on the wooden boards and closed my eyes. I whispered the serenity prayer and slowed my breathing. I held that memory in my mind, the warm sun escaping under the blind, the bodies around me, the safety of being in the hospital.

The land became my touchstone, the wide open paddocks, the scrub climbing the hill sides, the mountains, bald rock in the summer, snow-covered in winter. The birds building nests, the fledglings. The spring blooms, the leaf-covered summer trees, the stark, bare branches glistening with ice in winter. The Moon as She grew round and then became a whisper in the sky.

The horses became my family. I watched the pregnant belly of the mare and celebrated the birth of her foal. I witnessed his growth from gangly-legged yearling to cheeky colt. This progress continued until he completed his training and entered the dressage arena as a disciplined five-year-old.

While in my journal I slowly picked my life apart, stitch by stitch, until a patchwork of compartmentalised and normalised events lay in tatters around my feet. Years of denial. Years of hiding the truth. The end of the false life I'd created and added to over the years. All the lies and cover ups, self-deception and pointing the finger at someone else. And my role, always the victim.

I wrote about my fear of those in authority, the tone of their voice that reduced me to a child-like state and the control they had always held over my life. I wrote about my people-pleasing and the emotional need it satisfied. I wrote about the habitual hiding of who I was, out of fear of not being good enough or loveable. Because of self-hate. My heightened anxiety due to my uncontrollable temper, my fear of making decisions, of making mistakes or taking responsibility because of my overriding fear of being punished. The fear because it's always been physical.

I wrote about the child inside. I could feel her and imagine her. She's a tiny, curled little girl deep in my chest, burrowed beneath my breast bone. She's naked and alone, frightened and wounded. For so long She's managed my emotions and safeguarded my coping mechanisms. She's pretty much in charge, and I know She shouldn't be.

I carry Her fear with me into my adult life, my decisions, actions and reactions and behaviour. My instinct is to keep Her hidden although it causes apprehension and the fear someone will recognise me as the impostor I feel I am. In the past I've visualised Her in a cave, hidden deep within rock, such was my need to hide and protect Her. Now, I'm realising keeping her prisoner isn't doing either of us any good. She needs to be freed and given Her freedom to take Her place in my past, Her only remaining responsibility to be the little girl I was.

Eventually I left the farm, the country living, the land, the horses, the river and the mountains. I returned to the city, went to school, continued my creative writing and published my poems and short stories about my life. While doing this, I pursued repairing my relationship with my sons.

Sitting and listening to their pain, hearing about the hurt and anger I caused the two people I loved the most was the hardest part of my recovery and sobriety. It was distressing, humiliating and excruciatingly painful. But it was worth it. We have a new and honest relationships with each other, relationships that allowed me to attend their weddings and welcome my five grandchildren into my life.

They don't call me '*Mum*'. That woman ruined their childhood and left them to provide for themselves emotionally, physically and mentally. They were cast adrift at a very vulnerable time of their lives, on the brink of manhood, without the love and reassurance of a loving mother or parent. I understand my children's inability to forgive the mother who abandoned them. I am content to be recognised for who I am today; Hannah, a sober, wiser woman.

I want to break the cycle, the generational disease of addiction and co-dependence. I want to remain open to my own, my sons' and their children's understanding of trauma and the disease of addiction. I will never take for granted their ability to say, "I love you."

In talking with my eldest granddaughter about the book I suggested she might like to write something and these are the words she sent me.

Hannah Collins

To my grandmother.

I want to say thank you.

By sharing your story, I've always been encouraged to work on mine. While I don't think you know the full extent of that impact, you have been able to show me it's possible to acknowledge the tough parts inside and come out intact on the other side. I know it's not always sunshine and rainbows for anyone, but it's been nice to have someone in my eco-system that has gone out on a limb and done it a bit differently. By being open and honest about your life and journey, it's let me question some of those parts of me that I might have just lived with otherwise and reminded me that I don't have to be alone with my trauma.

As I get older and further through my own journey, I think we have more and more in common and more life lessons to share. You continue to be an inspiration and a reminder that despite all the bollocks, there is another side that looks pretty bright and happy.

So thank you for showing me not only what it has looked like, but what it can look like in the future. Thank you for continuing to work on yourself and talking about it honestly as a family member, as a woman and always as a human. Thank you for being a sounding board and always treating me with respect to give me the full picture so I have all the information to work with.

And lastly, thank you for still being here, for still listening to all the things I have to say, for welcoming me into your home and life regardless of time or distance, and for always loving me without condition.

With love from your eldest grandchild.

Postscript

This story wouldn't be complete without a fairy tale ending...

I fell in love with a red-head and moved to Sydney in 2010 to be with Heather. The following year we held our Commitment Ceremony with family and friends from New Zealand and Australia. When the 2018 plebiscite found in our favour, we married in April 2019.

Author Q & A

What is your motivation to write?
From my very first writings as a child I knew I would write about my life and share it with the world. My experience as a female in this male-organised world is no different from any other woman, however, given that my gift is Writing and my Soul Path Connection, I feel I'm able to give a voice to an experience where others mightn't have the language, or my words might stop others feeling alone and unheard. Perhaps also sharing this story might help someone to understand and heal.

What was your inspiration for Soul Connection?
To tell my story about healing from childhood sexual abuse, lesbian domestic violence and alcoholism and drug addiction. My childhood, and therefore my life, was defined by my paedophile grandfather. I was left angry, mistrustful, traumatised and afraid of the adult world. I was under the misconception that sex was love and those who professed to love you also hurt you. My use of alcohol and drugs escalated from social use to

addiction as the level of coercion, verbal and physical abuse increased. Although my children and I escaped from the relationship violence, as lives were never normal again. The story of my recovery from alcoholism and drug use has waited twenty-odd years to be told. I wanted to share my story to bring hope to those who need it, to give a voice to those who don't have one, and to tell women we can heal. We can be strong and move beyond the damage done to us and the self-harm we do to ourselves by believing we are worthless, unlovable and have no value to offer the world.

What do you want readers to take away from your story?
This is a story of hope and healing. I want to inspire women to share their story of recovery and sobriety, not just from alcoholism and drug addiction but from all the violence and abuse in our lives. We can rewrite our story and with self-love and self-forgiveness, live in gratitude.

About the author

Hannah Collins is a writer who writes exclusively about her life. She is a journaling junkie, a collector of notebooks, adult colouring books, note pads and creative greeting cards. She has been a passionate writer since childhood and always knew she'd self-publish her work. She has two adult sons and is grandmother to five grandchildren. She lives with her wife Heather, their four Chihuahuas, and cat George, in country Victoria.

Work in progress

'The Hidden Self - Healing Trauma' - a companion book workbook to 'Soul Connection'.

The Hidden Self is the Self that suffered trauma and remains frightened, ashamed and trapped. Using journaling, questions and exercises there's a way through the maze to the Hidden Self and healing.

You can contact Hannah: **https://hannahcollins.com.au/**
Facebook: **https://www.facebook.com/hannahcollinsauthor**

Acknowledgements

A special thanks to the wonderful women of the Newstead Writing Group who woke me up to the fact I had normalised the traumatic events in my life. Thank you all for your support throughout the writing of this book.

Thank you to my eldest granddaughter for sharing her thoughts, and to my wife Heather who every day gives me the love and support to write my story.

Once again to my wonderful publishing team, the professionals who make it possible for me to be an author.

Squarespace Website Designer & Brand Expert
Joanne has been a passionate graphic designer for over 15 years. As the creative director of Joanne Tapodi Creative she now specialises in building meaningful brands and intuitive websites for her clients.
https://www.joannetapodicreative.com.au/

Editing
Karen Crombie runs Exact Editing, where the aim is to make your work shine. After editing Hannah's first book, 'In Business Together', Karen is delighted to be working with her again to bring you 'Soul Connection'.
https://exactediting.com.au/

Typesetting
David is an experienced graphic designer, running his own design business for over a decade. In 2020, David was awarded Graphic Designer of the Year for Norfolk (UK) at the annual CorporateLiveWire Prestige Awards.
https://davidjameslawton.com/

Writing Coach
Emma Franklin Bell is an author, artist and mentor for creative people. Her flagship book coaching program Manuscript Mastery® has paved the way for many writers to become published authors in the business, inspirational and health and wellbeing space.
https://emmafranklinbell.com/

Photographer
CAPTURING MOMENTS THAT TELL YOUR STORY. From the enchanting innocence of a newborn, moments within a family or making a strong impression with professional headshots or business branding.
https://imagetechnique.com.au/

www.ingramcontent.com/pod-product-compliance
Lightning Source LLC
Chambersburg PA
CBHW020324010526
44107CB00054B/1974